WORKBOOK
KELLY PHILLIPS

BEGINNER
OUTCOMES

NATIONAL GEOGRAPHIC
LEARNING

ngl.cengage.com/outcomes

PASSWORD outcomes!C4#

NATIONAL GEOGRAPHIC
L E A R N I N G

National Geographic Learning,
a Cengage Company

Outcomes Beginner Workbook
Kelly Phillips

Vice President, Editorial Director:
John McHugh

Executive Editor: Siân Mavor

Editorial Project Manager: Laura Brant

Development Editor: Clare Shaw

Head of Strategic Marketing EMEA ELT:
Charlotte Ellis

Product Marketing Manager: Victoria Taylor

Head of Production and Design: Mike
Burggren

Content Project Manager: Ruth Moore

Manufacturing Manager: Eyvett Davis

Cover Design: Lisa Trager

Interior Design, Composition, and
Illustrations: QBS Learning

For permission to use material from this text or product,
submit all requests online at **cengage.com/permissions**
Further permissions questions can be emailed to
permissionrequest@cengage.com

Workbook and Audio CD
ISBN: 978-0-357-04224-3

National Geographic Learning
Cheriton House
North Way
Andover
UK
SP10 5BE

Locate your local office at **international.cengage.com/region**

Visit National Geographic Learning online at **ELTNGL.com**
Visit our corporate website at **www.cengage.com**

CREDITS

Although every effort has been made to contact copyright holders before publication, this has not always been possible. If contacted, the publisher will undertake to rectify any errors or omissions at the earliest opportunity.

Photos
5 (tl) © Estrada Anton/Shutterstock.com; 11 (tl) © meunierd/Shutterstock.com; 17 (tl) © gpointstudio/Shutterstock.com; 23 (tl) © Willy Barton/Shutterstock.com; 29 (tl) © TZIDO SUN/Shutterstock.com; 35 (tl) © Alf Ribeiro/Shutterstock.com; 41 (tl) © Dirima/Shutterstock.com; 47 (tl) © Dimasik_sh/Shutterstock.com; 53 (tl) © Monkey Business Images/Shutterstock.com; 59 (tl) © Olga Max/Shutterstock.com; 65 (tl) © sloukam/Shutterstock.com; 71 (tl) © Roman Babakin/Shutterstock.com; 4 (bl) © VGstockstudio/Shutterstock.com; 4 (br) © Hero Images/Getty Images; 5 (tl) © FS Productions/Blend Images/Getty Images; 5 (tl 1) © fatihhoca/E+/Getty Images; 5 (cl) © LightField Studios/Shutterstock.com; 5 (cr 1) © Beau Lark/Corbis/Getty Images; 5 (bl) © Monkey Business Images/Shutterstock.com; 4 (c) © HannaMonika/Shutterstock.com; 5 (tl 2) © Charlotte Purdy/Shutterstock.Com; 5 (tl 3) © Iakov Filimonov/Shutterstock.com; 5 (cr 2) © Kamil Macniak/Shutterstock.com; 5 (br 1) © WAYHOME studio/Shutterstock.com; 5 (br 2) © Odua Images/Shutterstock.com; 7 (tl) © Monkey Business Images/Shutterstock.com; 7 (cl) © oneinchpunch/Shutterstock.com; 7 (bl) © Tetiana Chernykova/Shutterstock.com; 8 (bl) © Odua Images/Shutterstock.com; 10 (br) © Milan Gonda/Shutterstock.com; 12 (tl) © Monkey Business Images/Shutterstock.com; 12 (tl) © YAKOBCHUK VIACHESLAV/Shutterstock.com; 12 (cl 1) © LightField Studios/Shutterstock.com; 12 (cr 1) © Syda Productions/Shutterstock.com; 12 (cl 2) © Alliance/Shutterstock.com; 12 (cr 2) © Gladskikh Tatiana/Shutterstock.com; 12 (bl) © Zurijeta/Shutterstock.com; 12 (br) © Minerva Studio/Shutterstock.com; 13 (bl) © Jenkedco/Shutterstock.com; 16 (tl) © Milan Stojanović/Dreamstime.com; 16 (tl) © Jackbluee/Dreamstime.com; 16 (cl) © John Arehart/Shutterstock.com; 16 (cr) © Lestertair/Shutterstock.com; 16 (bl) © olaser/E+/Getty Images; 16 (br) © Kosim Shukurov/Shutterstock.com; 17 (tl) © Nick Fox/Shutterstock.com; 17 (tl) © g-stockstudio/Shutterstock.com; 17 (bl) © Monkey Business Images/Shutterstock.com; 17 (br) © Roman Babakin/Shutterstock.com; 18 (tl) © Gabi Moisa/Shutterstock.com; 18 (cl) © Blend Images - KidStock/Brand X Pictures/Getty Images; 18 (bl) © Diego Cervo/Shutterstock.com; 20 (tl) © bitt24/Shutterstock.com; 20 (tc) © slobo/E+/Getty Images; 20 (tl) © sergign/Shutterstock.com; 20 (cl) © Nadezda/Shutterstock.com; 20 (cr) © Karkas/Shutterstock.com; 20 (bl) © Robert Red2000/Shutterstock.com; 20 (bc) © Terrance Emerson/Shutterstock.com; 20 (br) © Vangelis_Vassalakis/Shutterstock.com; 22 (tl) © Stuart Monk/Shutterstock.com; 22 (br) © Shuang Li/Shutterstock.com; 22 (tc) © Alastair Wallace/Shutterstock.com; 22 (cl) © VTT Studio/Shutterstock.com; 22 (c1) © Spotmatik Ltd/Shutterstock.com; 22 (c2) © Corepics VOF/Shutterstock.com; 22 (cr) © Peter Zurek/Shutterstock.com; 22 (bl) © Syda Productions/Shutterstock.com; 22 (bc 1) © Konstantin Romanov/Shutterstock.com; 22 (bc 2) © Kheng Guan Toh/Shutterstock.com; 23 (tl) © Gecko Studio/Shutterstock.com; 23 (b) © Bai-Bua's Dad/Shutterstock.com; 23 (tl) © Kingapl/Shutterstock.com; 25 (bc) © Loop Images/Universal Images Group/Getty Images; 27 (bl) © puhhha/Shutterstock.com; 29 (tl 1) © Takashi Images/Shutterstock.com; 29 (tl 2) © Daniel Hernanz Ramos/Moment/Getty Images; 29 (cr) © serdjophoto/Shutterstock.com; 29 (br 1) © Henryk T. Kaiser/Photolibrary/Getty Images; 29 (br 2) © Paolo Paradiso/Shutterstock.com; 30 (tl) © ICP/incamerastock/Alamy Stock Photo; 30 (tc) © PR Image Factory/Shutterstock.com; 30 (tl) © Gordon Bell/Shutterstock.com; 30 (bl) © Ceri Breeze/Shutterstock.com; 30 (bc) © Andrey_Popov/Shutterstock.com; 31 (tl) © oksana.perkins/Shutterstock.com; 31 (cr) © Sven Hansche/Shutterstock.com; 31 (bl) © SL-Photography/Shutterstock.com; 33 (cl) © Coast-to-Coast/iStock Editorial/Getty Images; 34 (tl) © Stokkete/Shutterstock.com; 34 (tl) © SpeedKingz/Shutterstock.com; 34 (cl) © Romolo Tavani/Shutterstock.com; 34 (cr) © Peshkova/Shutterstock.com; 34 (bl 2) © Elnur/Shutterstock.com; 34 (br) © Gubin Yury/Shutterstock.com; 35 (br) © Iakov Filimonov/Shutterstock.com; 36 (tl 1) © trebor/Alamy Stock Photo; 36 (tl 2) © S_Photo/Shutterstock.com; 36 (tl 3) © Berni/Shutterstock.com; 36 (cl 1) © Tatiana Bralnina/Shutterstock.com; 36 (cl 2) © PeJo29/iStock/Getty Images; 36 (bl 1) © Komar/Shutterstock.com; 36 (bl 3) © Rawpixel.com/Shutterstock.com; 36 (br) © nhungboon/Shutterstock.com; 37 (tl) © Radu Bercan/Shutterstock.com; 37 (cr) © happymay/Shutterstock.com; 37 (br) © chuyuss/Shutterstock.com; 39 (cl) © SONNY TUMBELAKA/AFP/Getty Images; 40 (tl) © Dmitriy Shironosov/Alamy Stock Photo; 40 (tl) © LightField Studios/Shutterstock.com; 40 (cl) © Golubovy/Shutterstock.com; 40 (cr) © Monkey Business Images/Shutterstock.com; 40 (bl) © bbernard/Shutterstock.com; 40 (br) © Africa Studio/Shutterstock.com; 40 (bc) © mama_mia/Shutterstock.com; 41 (tl) © a.collectionRF/amana images/Getty Images; 41 (cr) © Africa Studio/Shutterstock.com; 41 (br) © Syda Productions/Shutterstock.com; 43 (br) © Jacob Lund/Shutterstock.com; 44 (tl) © Surrphoto/Shutterstock.com; 44 (tl) © KKulikov/Shutterstock.com; 44 (cl) © Jr images/Shutterstock.com; 44 (cr) © Tarzhanova/iStock/Getty Images; 44 (tl) © mimagephotography/Shutterstock.com; 47 (bl) © mimagephotography/Shutterstock.com; 48 (br 2) © Luckeyman/Shutterstock.com; 48 (tl 1) © John And Penny/Shutterstock.com; 48 (tl 1) © Spaces Images/Blend Images/Getty Images; 48 (tl 2) © Alexandru Chiriac/Shutterstock.com; 48 (tl 2) © ROLAND ANCLA LEGASPI/Shutterstock.com; 48 (cl) © Emil Imarietli / Alamy Stock Photo; 48 (cr) © ben bryant/Shutterstock.com; 48 (bl 1) © ND700/Shutterstock.com; 48 (br 1) © Africa Studio/Shutterstock.com; 48 (bl 2) © DJ Srki/Shutterstock.com; 49 (tl) © Artazum/Shutterstock.com; 49 (cl 1) © iriana88w/Deposit Photos; 49 (cl 2) © Photographee.eu/Shutterstock.com; 49 (bl) © Milan Gonda/Alamy Stock Photo; 50 (tl) © wavebreakmedia/Shutterstock.com; 50 (tl) © Andrey_Popov/Shutterstock.com; 50 (cl) © Alexandr Gusev/Pacific Press/Alamy Stock Photo; 50 (cr) © New Africa/Shutterstock.com; 50 (bl) © El Nariz/Shutterstock.com; 50 (br) © wavebreakmedia/Shutterstock.com; 51 (tl) © Monkey Business Images/Shutterstock.com; 51 (bl) © Monkey Business Images/Shutterstock.com; 52 (tl) © Billion Photos/Shutterstock.com; 52 (tc) © Monkey Business Images/Shutterstock.com; 52 (tl) © mihailomilovanovic/iStock/Getty Images; 52 (bl) © BonNontawat/Shutterstock.com; 52 (br) © Rocketclips, Inc./Shutterstock.com; 55 (tl) © Milosz Maslanka/Shutterstock.com; 55 (bl) © etorres/Shutterstock.com; 55 (tl) © mikecranephotography.com/Alamy Stock Photo; 57 (cl) © Vikkin/Shutterstock.com; 59 (bc) © Gari Wyn Williams/Alamy Stock Photo; 60 (tl) © Christopher Boswell/Shutterstock.com; 60 (tl) © PhotoDisc/Getty Images; 60 (cl) © ERIC LAFFORGUE/Alamy Stock Photo; 60 (cr) © Christian Bertrand/Shutterstock.com; 60 (bl) © Ferenc Szelepcsenyi/Shutterstock.com; 61 (br) © Jeff J Mitchell/Getty Images; 67 (bl 1) © Library of Congress, Prints & Photographs Division, Reproduction number LC-USZ62-14759 (b&w film copy neg.); 67 (bl 2) © Universal History Archive/Getty Images; 68 (br) © Don Mammoser/Shutterstock.com; 72 (bl) © espies/Shutterstock.com; 72 (tl 2) © Lucie Lang/Shutterstock.com; 72 (tl 2) © Pavel_D/Shutterstock.com; 72 (br) © Dipak Shelare/Shutterstock.com; 72 (tl 1) © Ashley Whitworth/Shutterstock.com; 72 (tl 1) © Shebeko/Shutterstock.com; 72 (cl) © CYC/Shutterstock.com; 72 (cr) © Iurii Stepanov/Shutterstock.com; 72 (bc) © Phubes Juwattana/Shutterstock.com; 73 (cr) © Cucu Remus/Getty Images; 75 (tl) © MIXA/Getty Images.

Printed in Greece by Bakis S.A.
Print Number: 03   Print Year: 2020

CONTENTS

01 BE

VOCABULARY Numbers 1–12

1 Find the numbers 1–12 in the wordsquare. Look → and ↓.

G	J	T	F	I	V	E	U	J	G
G	S	W	E	E	T	J	S	X	I
A	B	E	J	Y	H	E	E	S	S
G	F	L	Q	K	R	K	L	T	I
O	V	V	K	S	E	V	E	N	X
D	F	E	H	O	E	F	V	W	T
G	T	W	O	O	N	E	E	I	E
T	C	Z	N	B	N	I	N	E	N
J	F	O	U	R	E	I	G	H	T
A	E	Y	X	K	R	H	G	C	Z

2 🕭 1.1 Listen and circle the numbers you hear.

1 2 ③ 4 5 6 7 8 9 10 11 12

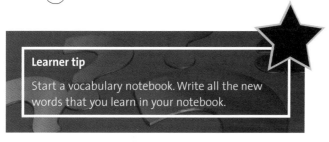

Learner tip

Start a vocabulary notebook. Write all the new words that you learn in your notebook.

LISTENING

3 🕭 1.2 Listen to the conversation and tick (✓) the correct picture (1 or 2).

1 ☐

2 ☐

4 🕭 1.2 Listen again and number the sentences in the correct order.

Ines, this is my friend Ethan.	[ ]
Hi. I'm Ines.	[ ]
Hi. Nice to meet you.	[ ]
Khalid.	[ ]
Nice to meet you.	[ ]
What's your name?	[1]
Yes. You, too, Ines.	[ ]
Yes. You, too.	[ ]

DEVELOPING CONVERSATIONS
Checking names

5 Read the conversations. Circle the correct words.
1 A: Who's *he* / *she*?   B: He's Greg.
2 A: Who's she?   B: *He's* / *She's* Lara.
3 A: Who are *he* / *they*?   B: Leo and Sue.
4 A: Who's he?   B: *I* / *He* don't know.

6 Complete the conversations with the words and phrases in the box.

are they	I	know	's he	's she	Who

1 A: Who's he?
   B: *I* don't know.
2 A: Who.............................. ?
   B: She's Emma.
3 A: Who.............................. ?
   B: He's Ben.
4 A: Who .... ?
   B: Tina and Jack.
5 A: Who's he?
   B: I don't ....
6 A: .... are they?
   B: Hugh and Poppy.

VOCABULARY People

7 Look at the photos. Put the letters in the correct order and write the words.

1 cdorot *doctor*

2 reetcha ....

3 ndfrie ....

4 nso ....

5 therom ....

6 ifwe ....

8 Complete the words for people with the vowels (a, e, i, o, u).

1 f a th e r
2 d _ _ ght _ r
3 br _ th _ r
4 h _ sb _ nd
5 s _ st _ r

9 ♺ 1.3 Listen. Complete the sentences. Use words from Exercises 7 and 8.

1 Shirley: Liam is my *husband*. He's a doctor.
2 Liam: Shirley is my wife. She's a ....
in an English school. This is my son, Hugh. He's nine. And she is my ...., Rebeca. She's nine, too!
3 Rebeca: Hugh's my .... He is my best ...., too. We're in the same class at school!
4 Hugh: Rebeca is my sister. My .... is a teacher and my .... is a doctor.

GRAMMAR 'm, 's, 're

10 Complete the sentences with 'm, 's, 're or is.

1 He*'s* my husband.
2 Hi, I.......................... Oliver.
3 My name .... Sophia.
4 She.......................... a teacher.
5 They.......................... nice!
6 This .... my brother, Lucas.
7 We.......................... your friends.
8 You.......................... my doctor, right?

11 Look at the pictures and complete the sentences. Use the words from the box.

He's	I'm	She's	They're	~~We're~~

1 *We're* Poppy and Maria.
2 .... James.
3 .... Katia.
4 .... Andrew.
5 .... Zoe and Stella.

VOCABULARY Numbers 13–22

1 🔊 **1.4 Listen and circle the numbers you hear.**

18	15	21	4	17	22	13	16

14	3	10	12	19	8	20	9

2 🔊 **1.4 Listen and repeat.**

Language note

Use a hyphen (-) when you write numbers after 20, for example, twenty-one and twenty-two.

3 Find the numbers 13–22 in the wordsnake.

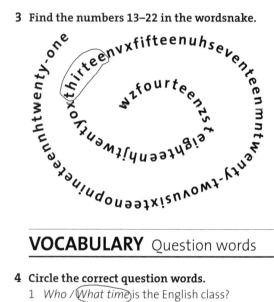

VOCABULARY Question words

4 Circle the correct question words.
1 *Who / What time* is the English class?
2 *How old / How long* is your son?
3 *How much / Who* is lunch?
4 *Who / What time* is she?
5 *How old / Where* are you from?
6 *Who / How long* is the class?

5 Complete the conversations with question words.
1 A: *Where* is Paola from?
   B: She's from Brazil.
2 A: .... is the party?
   B: 9 o'clock.
3 A: .... is the coffee break?
   B: Fifteen minutes.
4 A: .... is this pen?
   B: Two euros.
5 A: .... are you?
   B: I'm twenty-two.
6 A: .... is he?
   B: He's my doctor.

GRAMMAR Questions with *be*

6 Read the questions. Circle the correct words.
1 Where *are* / *is* Elena and Niko from?
2 How old *is* / *are* Jack?
3 How long *are* / *is* the break?
4 What time *are* / *is* the class?
5 *Are* / *Is* they nice?
6 Who *are* / *is* they?
7 How much *are* / *is* coffee?
8 *Is* / *Are* you OK?

7 Write questions with these words.
1 what time / the break   *What time is the break?*
2 how much / the books   ....
3 how / you   ....
4 the coffee / nice   ....
5 who / he   ....
6 where / Akemi from   ....
7 how old / Ava   ....
8 how long / the classes   ....

8 Match the answers (a–h) with the questions (1–8) in Exercise 7.
a One hour.   ....
b Yes, it's good!   ....
c He's my son.   ....
d Japan.   ....
e 11 o'clock.   *1*
f Nine pounds.   ....
g I'm OK, thanks.   ....
h She's 19.   ....

GRAMMAR *his, her, our, their*

9 Match (1–4) with (a–d).
1 Helen's doctor   a their doctor
2 Tom's doctor   b his doctor
3 Elena and George's doctor   c her doctor
4 Noah's and my doctor   d our doctor

10 Complete the text with the words in the box.

her	his	our	their

Hi! I'm Lucy and this is my husband, Dan. This is
¹ .... flat. This is Frank and this is ² ....
wife, Regan. Frank and Regan are English and
³ .... flat is in Oxford. This is Maria and this is
⁴ .... mother, Lily.

11 The words in bold are wrong. Write the correct words.

1 This is my sister, Nancy. This is **his** mother.   *her*

2 This is Gina and **Ethan** teacher.   ....

3 This is Harry and this is Pamela. This
is **our** flat.   ....

4 This is **Sharons** father.   ....

5 I'm Ken and this is my sister. This is
their doctor.   ....

READING

12 Look at the photos and read the invitations. Match the photos (1–3) with the parties (a–c).

1

2

3

a

ARIA AND TINA HAVE A NEW FLAT

Come to their party

at Flat 12, Floor 5, 19 Elm Street

This Friday (14ᵗʰ) 4pm – 7pm

Their phone number is 131 845 2667.

b

JOE HAS A NEW BABY BROTHER!

Come to our party!

Flat 21, Floor 2, 13 Oak Street

| Friday 19th, 1pm – 4pm | Lunch at 3pm! |

Mobile: 08792 627 4790
Morgan, Sian and Joe

c

I'm 21!

Come to my party at:

Sam's Restaurant, 18 Brown Street

Saturday 18ᵗʰ 8pm – 11pm

Camila

My phone number is 131 767 7529.

13 Read about the parties again. Are these sentences true or false? Circle T or F.

1 Aria and Tina have a new flat.   (T)   F

2 Aria and Tina's party is on Sunday.   T   F

3 Tina and Joe have a new baby.   T   F

4 Morgan's number is 08792 627 4790.   T   F

5 Camila's party is at her flat.   T   F

6 Camila's party is on Saturday.   T   F

14 Circle the correct words. Then answer the questions.

1 *Who /* (How long) *is Aria and Tina's party?*
Three hours.

2 *What / Where* time is Aria and Tina's party?
....

3 *How / What* day is Morgan and Sian's party?
....

4 *Who / How* is Joe?
....

5 *How / Where* old is Camila?
....

6 *Who / Where's* Camila's party?
....

VOCABULARY Times and prices

1 Complete the words for numbers with the vowels (a, e, i, o, u).

e i ghty   f__fty-s__v__n   n__n__ty-s__x   f__rty
s__v__nty   s__xty-thr__ __   th__rty-tw__   tw__nty

2 Read the sentences. Are they times (T) or prices (P)? Circle T or P.

1 Our break is at ten thirty.   (T)   P
2 A coffee is €2.99.   T   P
3 Cake is three pounds fifty.   T   P
4 It's 2pm.   T   P
5 My English class is at three o'clock.   T   P
6 Lunch is $9.99.   T   P

Learner tip

A *currency* is a kind of money. Write these words for currencies in your vocabulary notebook:
$ = dollar   £ = pound   € = euro

PRONUNCIATION Numbers

3 🔊 1.5 Listen and tick (✓) the number you hear, a or b.

1 a 13   [ ]   b 30   [✓]
2 a 8   [ ]   b 18   [ ]
3 a $19.99   [ ]   b $90.99   [ ]
4 a 14   [ ]   b 40   [ ]
5 a €17.50   [ ]   b €7.50   [ ]

4 🔊 1.5 Listen and repeat.

VOCABULARY In a coffee shop

5 Circle the word that is different in each group.

1 americano   cappuccino   (sandwich)
2 cake   espresso   latte
3 medium   tea   large
4 orange juice   water   small
5 sandwich   large   cake

DEVELOPING CONVERSATIONS
Ordering and serving drinks

6 Complete the conversation with the words in the box.

anything	else	like	much	thanks	~~would~~

A: What ¹ *would* you ² .... ?
B: How ³ .... is a small orange juice?
A: Three ninety-nine.
B: OK. A small orange juice, please.
A: Orange juice. Anything ⁴ .... ?
B: Yes – a coffee cake, please.
A: OK. ⁵ .... else?
B: No, ⁶ ....
A: That's seven ninety-nine.

7 🔊 1.6 Listen and check.

GRAMMAR not

8 Write *not* in the correct place.

        not
1 My sandwich – it's ∧ right.

2 It's a chocolate cake.

3 It's small – medium.

4 My cappuccino – it's hot.

5 A latte is £3.69 – £5.69!

9 Write the words in the correct order to make sentences.

1 not / It's / right
   It's not right.
2 small / not / It's
   ....
3 a coffee cake / not / It's
   ....
4 pounds / It's / five / not
   ....
5 not / is / hot / My americano
   ....

LISTENING

10 🔊 1.7 Listen to the conversation. Where are the people? Tick (✓) the correct answer.

a at a party   [ ]
b at a coffee shop   [ ]
c at a class   [ ]

11 🔊 **1.7 Listen again and circle the correct words.**

A: ¹ *Thanks / Hi*, what would you like, sir?

B: How much is a large ² *cake / latte*?

A: ³ *Four fifty / Four fifteen*.

B: OK. A large latte, please.

A: Anything else?

B: Yes – a chocolate cake, please.

A: Thank you! ... Here you are. Is everything OK?

B: No. My latte – it's not right.

A: What's the problem, sir?

B: This is a ⁴ *large / small* latte – not a ⁵ *large / medium*.

A: Oh, yes. Sorry. OK. That's ⁶ *nine nineteen / nine ninety*.

12 Tick (✓) what the man ordered.

1 a small latte	[ ]	3 a coffee cake	[ ]
2 a chocolate cake	[ ]	4 a large latte	[ ]

DEVELOPING WRITING Describing people

13 Circle the CAPITAL letters in the sentences.

1 Come to our party at 3 High Street.

2 This is my daughter, Poppy.

3 Hi, I'm Lara.

4 He's from São Paulo in Brazil.

5 This is our son, David.

14 When do we use capital letters? Choose ✓ or ✗.

1 names of people	[✓]
2 times	[ ]
3 names of streets	[ ]
4 prices	[ ]
5 cities	[ ]
6 countries	[ ]
7 the first word in a sentence	[ ]
8 the word *I*	[ ]

15 Tick the people in your life. Choose three people and write sentences. What are their names? How old are they?

friend(s)	[ ]	father	[ ]
brother(s)	[ ]	mother	[ ]
sister(s)	[ ]	husband	[ ]
daughter(s)	[ ]	wife	[ ]
son(s)	[ ]		

My friends are Ava and Juan. They are 15 and 17.

My father is Abdul. He's 52.

....

....

....

....

....

....

Vocabulary Builder Quiz 1

Download the Vocabulary Builder for Unit 1 and try the quiz below. Write your answers in your notebook. Then check them and record your score.

1 Are the words for food (F) or drinks (D)? Circle F or D.

1	tea	F	D
2	sandwich	F	D
3	cake	F	D
4	milk	F	D
5	chocolate	F	D
6	water	F	D
7	coffee	F	D

2 Write the words in the box in the correct place.

brother	daughter	invitation	school
Sunday	wife		

1 husband   ....

2 son   ....

3 party   ....

4 sister   ....

5 Saturday   ....

6 teacher   ....

3 Circle the correct words.

1 That's a big *flat / Friday*.

2 Yes, that's *same / right*.

3 I don't *like / know*.

4 What's your *name / doctor*?

5 Nice to *meet / come* you!

6 A fresh orange *cappuccino / juice*, please.

4 Complete the words in the sentences with the vowels (*a, e, i, o, u*).

1 Where are you fr__m?

2 Gina is in my English cl__ss.

3 Stavros is my best fr____nd.

4 How long is the br____k?

5 __nyth__ng else?

6 How much is a m__d____m espresso?

Score ___/25

Wait a couple of weeks and try the quiz again.
Compare your scores.

LIVE, WORK, EAT

VOCABULARY My home

1 Find nine words related to people's homes in the wordsnake.

2 Look at the pictures and numbers 1–8. Write words from Exercise 1 next to the correct number.

1 village
2 ....
3 ....
4 ....
5 ....
6 ....
7 ....
8 ....

1 *village*

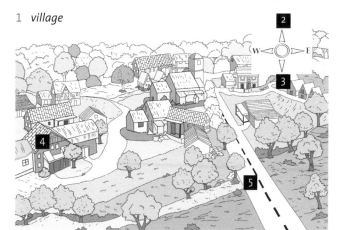

6 ....

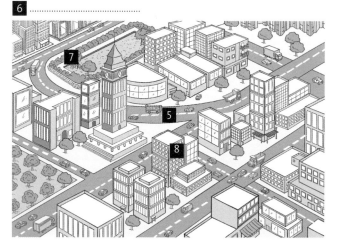

GRAMMAR Present simple

3 Choose the correct words.
1 They *walk* / *walks* on the road to the centre.
2 It *take* / *takes* twenty minutes.
3 I *lives* / *live* in a village.
4 She *has* / *have* a small house.
5 You *has* / *have* a big flat.
6 We *like* / *likes* the centre.
7 He's from Ottawa. He *know* / *knows* the city.

> **Language note**
> -
> *I / you / we / they* **have**, but *he / she / it* **has**.

4 Complete the sentences with the present simple form of the verbs in brackets.
1 My brother **knows** Peter. They're friends. (know)
2 My mother and father ....
   in a small village. (live)
3 We .... you. You're in our class! (know)
4 I .... their flat. It's big. (like)
5 You .... two parks in your city. (have)
6 We walk to school. It ....
   five minutes. (take)
7 My friend Maria .... in Chile. (live)

5 Complete the text with the words in the box.

| has | have | knows | ~~like~~ | likes | lives |

My name is Stella and this is my city, Athens. I ¹ *like* my city. Athens ² .... houses, flats, roads – and nice parks! I ³ .... a brother. His name's Spyros. He ⁴ .... in a small village called Kastania with his wife, Sophia. He ⁵ .... his village – it's great! He ⁶ .... the people in the village.

GRAMMAR

Present simple questions: *do you*

6 Choose the correct words.
1 *Do you like / You like* your village?
2 *Who you live / Who do you live* with?
3 *You do have / Do you have* a flat or a house?
4 *Where is / Where do* you live?
5 *Do you know / Do you knows* my father?
6 *Do you walk / You walk* here?

7 Match the answers (a–f) with the questions (1–6) in Exercise 6.
a   A flat.   [   ]
b   My wife and baby son.   [   ]
c   Yes. He's my doctor.   [   ]
d   On Hill Road.   [   ]
e   Yes. It takes ten minutes.   [   ]
f   Yes. It's nice and has a big park.   [1]

8 Read the conversations. Write questions using the words. Use a question word in questions 4–6.
1 A: you / live with your mother and father
   Do you live with your mother and father?
   B: Yes. And my sister.
2 A: you / like my husband's village
   ....?
   B: Yes. It's nice.
3 A: you / have a big house
   ....?
   B: No. It's small.
4 A: you / live
   ....?
   B: I live on Elm Road.
5 A: you / know here
   ....?
   B: I know Ines and Khalid.
6 A: you / have a flat
   ....?
   B: I have a flat in Rio.

DEVELOPING CONVERSATIONS

And you?

9 Number the parts of each conversation 1–3.
1 I'm twenty. And you?   [*2*]
   I'm eighteen.   [*3*]
   How old are you?   [*1*]
2 I'm great.   [   ]
   Fine, thanks. And you?   [   ]
   How are you?   [   ]
3 Caleb. And you?   [   ]
   Marianna.   [   ]
   What's your name?   [   ]

10 Complete the conversations with the answers in the box.

I'm OK.	Near the park.	No, it's very big.
Suki.	Yes, a sister.	

1 A: How are you?   B: Fine, thanks. And you?
   A: *I'm OK.*
2 A: What's your name?   B: Cristiano. And you?
   A: ....
3 A: Where do you live?   B: On Grant Road. And you?
   A: ....
4 A: Do you have a brother or sister?
   B: A brother. And you?
   A: ....
5 A: Do you like London?   B: Yes, it's great. And you?
   A ....

LISTENING

11 ⦿ 2.1 Listen to the conversation. Tick (✓) the things the people talk about.
1 names   [✓]   5 brothers and sisters [   ]
2 times   [   ]   6 mothers and fathers   [   ]
3 prices   [   ]   7 friends   [   ]
4 homes   [   ]

12 ⦿ 2.1 Listen again. Circle the correct words.
Angelina:
1 lives *on Venice Road* / *in Westville*.
2 lives near *Sebastian* / *their school*.
3 *walks* / *takes a bus* to school.

Sebastian:
4 lives in *a flat* / *a house*.
5 has a *big* / *small* home.
6 lives with his *mother and father* / *friends*.

VOCABULARY Jobs

1 Put the letters in the correct order. Write the jobs next to the correct photos (a–h).

1	usb ridrev	5	nttsued
2	mmu	6	eahcetr
3	serun	7	tiware
4	erdtier	8	rokw ni na iceffo

a *bus driver*

b ....

c ....

d ....

e ....

f ....

g ....

h ....

Learner tip

Learn new words every day. Have a friend test you. It's a great way to remember new words.

GRAMMAR Present simple: *don't (do not)*

2 Write the words in the correct order to make sentences.

1 in / I / a / live / flat / don't
I don't live in a flat.

2 big / don't / cities / They / like
....

3 don't / to / go / school / We
....

4 have / don't / You / job / a
....

5 an / don't / in / office / They / work
....

3 Write three sentences that are true for you. Use *don't*.

....
....
....

GRAMMAR Plural / no plural

4 Are the words correct? Write (✓) or (✗).

1	doctors	[✓]	6	waters	[ ]
2	jobs	[ ]	7	persons	[ ]
3	childs	[ ]	8	teachers	[ ]
4	moneys	[ ]	9	waiters	[ ]
5	hours	[ ]			

Language note

Most nouns form their plural with *s*.
road – roads   mother – mothers
Some plurals are irregular.
*child – children (*childs*)   person – **people** (*peoples*)*

5 Write the plurals of the words. Write (✗) for words with no plural.

1	nurse	*nurses*	6	flat	....
2	child	....	7	work	....
3	student	....	8	drink	....
4	money	....	9	mum	....
5	person	....	10	area	....

6 The words in bold are wrong. Write the correct words.

1 I am a bus driver. The money **are** good.   *is*
2 We don't have a lot of **times**.   ....
3 This is my school. The people **is** nice.   ....
4 The **house** are small.   ....
5 Some nurses **is** great.   ....
6 James has two **flat**.   ....

READING

7 Read the four texts. Where do the people live? Write the country.

1 Loretta ....
2 Juan ....
3 Channary ....
4 Hans ....

8 Are the sentences true or false? Circle T or F.

1 Loretta's job is in the north of Toronto. T (F)
2 Loretta works with nice people. T F
3 Juan works in a small school. T F
4 Juan likes his students. T F
5 Channary works in an office. T F
6 Channary lives in a big city. T F
7 Hans lives with three people. T F
8 Hans has a lot of free time. T F

 WORK IN A DIFFERENT COUNTRY!

December 13
STAR RATING ★ ★ ★ ✶

Hi, I'm Loretta. I'm from New Zealand, but now I live and work in Toronto, Canada. I live in an area called Scarborough. I work in an office in the south of the city. It takes 20 minutes by bus. The job's OK. I like the people I work with, but the money is bad.

December 19
STAR RATING ★ ★ ✶

Hello. I'm Juan. I'm from Spain, but I'm a teacher in Leeds, England. My job's OK, but I don't like the school. It's big and it's in the centre. It's 50 minutes by train from my flat. The students are great, but I don't like some classes.

December 21
STAR RATING ★ ★ ★ ★

Hello. My name's Channary. I'm from Cambodia. Now I live and work in Sweden. I work for a bus company. I'm a bus driver. I like my job. Traffic isn't bad in Avesta – it's a small city. The money is good and I don't work a lot of hours – 15 a week. I have lots of time with my friends and my two dogs!

December 30
STAR RATING ★ ★ ★ ★

My name's Hans. I'm from Germany, but now I live and work in Poland – in an area in the north of Warsaw. I live in a house with three people from different countries. I'm a waiter. It's OK. I like the other waiters, but I don't like the hours. I go to work from 4 to 9. And I have classes too, from 8 to 3. That's a lot of hours!

DEVELOPING WRITING
Writing a description of yourself

Acacia's blog

Profile

1 [*a*] Acacia Gonzales

2 [ ] 19

3 [ ] **From:** Mexico

4 [ ] **Live in:** Comitán (city); Chiapas (area); in the south of Mexico

5 [ ] **Home:** flat

6 [ ] **Live with:** my mother and father

7 [ ] Student at Instituto Tecnológico

9 Read Acacia's profile on her blog. Match the information (1–7) to the questions (a–g).

a What's your name?
b Where do you live?
c How old are you?
d Where are you from?
e Do you live in a house or a flat?
f What do you do?
g Who do you live with?

10 Complete the blog with information about Acacia.

Hi, I'm [1] *Acacia Gonzales*. I'm [2] ....
I'm from [3] ....

I live in a city called [4] ....
It's in an area called [5] .... ,
in the [6] .... of Mexico.

I live in a small flat with [7] .... It's on a big road, near a small park. I don't work. I go to a university called [8] ....

11 Answer the questions in Exercise 9 about yourself. Write a blog profile for you.

VOCABULARY Food and drinks

1 Circle the word that is different in each group.

1 burger	chicken	(orange juice)
2 salad	ice cream	cake
3 meat	fish	drinks
4 vegetables	salad	coffee cake
5 water	meat	fruit juice

2 Look at the pictures and complete the crossword.

```
[1]        [2]
 J   U  I   C   E
              [3]      [4]
                    
                    
                    
          [5]         
```

Across →

1   3   5

Down ↓

2   3   4

GRAMMAR like / don't like

3 Complete the sentences with like ☺, don't like ☹ or love ❤.

1 I **don't like** meat. ☹
2 Burgers and chips! I .... them! ❤
3 I .... tea and coffee. ☺
4 Fish? No, thanks. I .... it. ☹
5 I .... ice cream! ☺
6 I .... fresh fruit and salads. ❤

4 Complete the sentences with like, don't like or love so they are true for you.

1 I .... fruit.
2 I .... fish and seafood.
3 I .... vegetarian dishes.
4 I .... carrot cake.
5 I .... cheese pizza.
6 I .... bacon sandwiches.

5 Complete the conversations with it or them.

1 A: I love ice cream.
   B: Me, too. I love *it*!
2 A: I love burgers.
   B: Me, too. I love .... with chips.
3 A: I don't like strawberries.
   B: I don't like ...., but I like oranges.
4 A: I don't like bacon.
   B: Oh? I love ....
5 A: I like fruit juice.
   B: Yes, I like ...., too.
6 A: I like kebabs.
   B: No! I don't like ....!

DEVELOPING CONVERSATIONS
Ordering food

6 Write the words in the correct order to make sentences from a conversation in a restaurant. Who says the sentence, the waiter (W) or a customer (C)?

1 with / else / your fish? / Anything
Anything else with your fish?   [*W*]

2 order? / Are you / to / ready   [   ]
....

3 please. / Chips,   [   ]
....

4 please. / fish, / The   [   ]
....

5 much / a salad? / is / How   [   ]
....

6 you? / And   [   ]
....

7 pounds. / ten / It's   [   ]
....

8 thanks. / Oh! / No,   [   ]
....

9 rice / or chips? / With   [   ]
....

10 with chips / A burger / for me / Yes.   [   ]
....

7 Put the sentences from Exercise 6 in the correct order. Write the conversation.

W: *Are you ready to order?*
C: ....
W: ....
C: ....
W: ....
C: ....
W: ....
C: ....
W: ....
C: ....

8 ⏺ 2.2 Listen and check your answers.

LISTENING

9 🔊 **2.3 Listen to four conversations. Match the conversations (1–4) to the pictures (a–d).**

10 🔊 **2.3 Listen again. Are the sentences true or false? Circle T or F.**

Conversation 1
1 The woman likes espresso.   T   F
2 The woman likes tea.   T   F
Conversation 2
3 The boy loves cake and ice cream. T   F
4 The boy doesn't like vegetables.   T   F
Conversation 3
5 The man wants a table for two.   T   F
6 The people don't know English.   T   F
Conversation 4
7 A coke is five euros thirteen.   T   F
8 The man says the coke is expensive. T   F

PRONUNCIATION /z/ and /s/

11 **Read these words and think about the sound of the letters in bold. What are the two different sounds?**

bu**s** driver	doctor**s**	doe**s**	flat**s**
hour**s**	hou**s**e	live**s**	**s**outh

12 🔊 **2.4 Listen and write the words in the correct place.**

/z/	/s/
....	*bus driver*
....	....
....	....
....	....

13 🔊 **2.4 Listen again and check your answers.**

Vocabulary Builder Quiz 2

Download the Vocabulary Builder for Unit 2 and try the quiz below. Write your answers in your notebook. Then check them and record your score.

1 **Are the words for people (P) or places (PL)? Circle P or PL.**
   1 city   P   PL
   2 village   P   PL
   3 driver   P   PL
   4 nurse   P   PL
   5 centre   P   PL
   6 waiter   P   PL
   7 student   P   PL

2 **Circle the word that is different in each group.**
   1 great   expensive   good
   2 train   taxi   person
   3 bacon   chicken   carrot
   4 salad   ice cream   tomato
   5 minute   burger   meat
   6 office   dog   shop

3 **Write the words in the box in the correct place.**

chips	dad	far	small	south	vegetables

   1 fruit and   ....
   2 north and   ....
   3 mum and   ....
   4 big and   ....
   5 near and   ....
   6 fish and   ....

4 **Complete the words in the sentences with the vowels (a, e, i, o, u).**
   1 I l__v__ with two friends.
   2 I don't like my job. I work a lot of h__ __rs.
   3 Westville is in an __r__ __ called Pictou County.
   4 Do you have a h__ __s__ or a flat?
   5 I don't work. I'm r__t__r__d.
   6 The __n__v__rs__ty is on Brant Road.

Score ___/25

Wait a couple of weeks and try the quiz again.
Compare your scores.

03 LOVE, WANT, NEED

VOCABULARY Adjectives

1 Match the adjectives (1–4) with their opposites (a–d).

1 bad   a hot
2 big   b small
3 cold   c old
4 new   d good

> **Learner tip**
>
> When you learn new adjectives, write them with their opposites (≠).

2 Complete the adjectives with the vowels (*a, e, i, o, u*).

1 d*iffic*ult
2 __xp__ns__v__
3 gr__ __t
4 h__ngry
5 m__rr__ __d
6 n__c__
7 t__r__d
8 w__ll

3 Look at the photos and the sentences. Circle the correct word. Then complete the sentence with *a* or *an*.

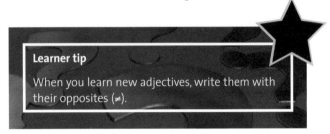

1 It's *a* cold / (hot) pizza.
2 It's .... *big / married* house.
3 It's .... *old / new* flat.
4 He's .... *small / hungry* man.
5 It's .... *difficult / expensive* coffee shop.
6 He's .... *tired / new* man.

Language note

Vowels are *a, e, i, o, u*. All the other letters in the alphabet are consonants.
We use *a* before words which start with a consonant.
a big city, **a n**ew flat
We use *an* before words which start with a vowel.
an old house, **an E**nglish class

PRONUNCIATION
Saying words together

4 🔊 3.1 Listen. Which two words sound like one word? Draw lines.

1 an_expensive flat
2 an orange bus
3 an English teacher
4 an old village

5 🔊 3.1 Listen again and repeat.

GRAMMAR Negatives with *be*

6 Circle the correct words.

1 She *'m not* / ('s not) my teacher.
2 They *'re not* / *'s not* expensive flats.
3 We *'re not* / *'m not* from China.
4 I *'re not* / *'m not* tired.
5 It *'re not* / *'s not* a big hotel.

7 The words in bold are incorrect. Write the correct words.

1 It**'re not** a very good coffee shop.   *'s not*
2 We**'m not** very well. ....
3 He**'re not** married, right? ....
4 They**'m not** new students. ....
5 I**'re not** your waiter. ....

8 Complete the conversations with *'m not, 's not* or *'re not*.

1 A: Your room is great!
   B: Thanks. And it**'s not** expensive.
2 A: Do you know Maria and Tia?
   B: No, they .... in my class.
3 A: Do you know the city?
   B: No, we .... from here.
4 A: Is Ella his wife?
   B: No, he .... married.
5 A: Do you want a sandwich?
   B: No, thanks. I .... very hungry.

LISTENING

9 🔊 **3.2 Listen to four conversations. Match the pictures (a–d) with the conversations (1–4).**

a

b

c

d

10 🔊 **3.2 Listen again. Number the questions in the correct order.**

a   How's the weather?   [   ]
b   How's your son?   [   ]
c   How's your job?   [   ]
d   How's your flat?   [   ]

11 Complete the sentences from the conversations with the words in the box.

difficult   expensive   hot   very good   ~~very well~~

Conversation 1
1 A: He's not *very well*.
   B: Oh, no! I'm sorry.
Conversation 2
2 A: It's good, but flats in the city are ....
   B: Yes!
Conversation 3
3 A: It's very .... I love it.
   B: Oh. It's not normally hot in Canada.
Conversation 4
4 A: It's not .... How's your job?
   B: The same. And it's ....!

12 🔊 **3.2 Listen again and check your answers.**

DEVELOPING CONVERSATIONS
Responding to news

13 Complete the table with the sentences in the box.

~~It's very cold here.~~	My chicken's not hot.
She's very well, thanks.	His job is difficult.
It's very nice.	The other students are great.

Good news ☺	Bad news ☹
....	*It's very cold here.*
....	....
....	....
....	....

14 Complete the conversations with the sentences in Exercise 13.

1 A: How's the weather in Moscow?
   B: I don't like it. *It's very cold here.*
2 A: How's your brother?
   B: He's very tired. ....
      And the money's not very good.
3 A: How's your sister?
   B: Leah? ....
4 A: How's your food?
   B: It's very bad. ....
5 A: How's university?
   B: I love it! ....
6 A: How's your hotel?
   B: .... And it's new!

15 Respond to the news in Exercise 14. Write *Oh, good* or *I'm sorry* for each conversation.

Conversation 1:	*I'm sorry.*
Conversation 2:	....
Conversation 3:	....
Conversation 4:	....
Conversation 5:	....
Conversation 6:	....

VOCABULARY *go, take, want*

> **Learner tip**
>
> We use some verbs in English a lot. When you learn verbs like *go*, *take* and *want*, try to learn some of the nouns that we use them with, too.

1 The words in bold are incorrect. Write the correct words (*goes, takes* or *wants*).

1 My father **goes** a shower every day.   *takes*
2 Anna **wants** shopping on Saturday.   ....
3 My brother is hungry. He **goes** a salad.   ....
4 He **takes** to the park on Friday.   ....
5 The bus **wants** a long time.   ....
6 The baby **goes** some milk.   ....
7 My sister **goes** the train to school.   ....

2 Complete the texts with *goes, takes* or *wants*.

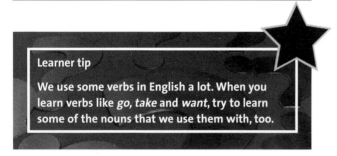

My friend, Muhammed, [1] *takes* the bus every day. He [2] .... to the gym. He [3] .... a shower every day, too. He [4] .... a long time.

My sister [5] .... shopping every day. She [6] .... to buy new clothes. They are expensive! She [7] .... to the coffee shop every day, too. She [8] .... to meet her friends.

Helen loves hot weather. She [9] .... to Cuba – she [10] .... on holiday. She [11] .... photos. Her photos are great!

GRAMMAR Present simple: *doesn't*

3 Make the sentences negative.

1 He likes fish.
   He doesn't like fish.
2 Leo knows my teacher.
   ....
3 The train takes a long time.
   ....
4 My brother wants to go to the party.
   ....
5 The bus goes to the city.
   ....
6 She lives in a new house.
   ....

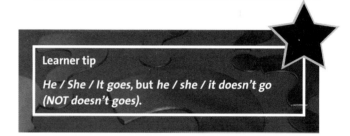

> **Learner tip**
>
> *He / She / It goes*, but *he / she / it doesn't go* (NOT *doesn't goes*).

4 Write the words in the correct order to make sentences.

1 the / doesn't / train / She / take
   She doesn't take the train.
2 hotel / He / like / doesn't / his
   ....
3 go / doesn't / shopping / every day / Maria
   ....
4 have / doesn't / My mother / car / a
   ....
5 to / long / doesn't / walk / school / to / It / take
   ....
6 doesn't / my / near / gym / The number 10 bus / go
   ....

5 Complete the conversations with the verbs.

1 A: My friend *wants* a pizza. She's hungry.   (want)
   B: My friend's not hungry.
      He .... to eat.   (not want)
2 A: My brother .... two
      daughters.   (have)
   B: That's nice. My brother ....
      children.   (not have)
3 A: My mother .... the bus
      to work.   (take)
   B: My mother .... the bus.   (not like)
4 A: The train .... a long time
      to get to the centre.   (take)
   B: I know. My father .... it.   (not take)

GRAMMAR
Present simple questions: *does*

6 Match the questions (1–6) with the answers (a–f).

1 What does your brother do?   [*f*]
2 Why does she want a big house?   [   ]
3 How long does it take to get to the city? [   ]
4 Where does your sister work?   [   ]
5 How does he come to school?   [   ]
6 Does she have any children?   [   ]

a In an office.   d Twenty minutes.
b He walks.   e Yes, a son and a
c She wants a lot of   daughter.
    children!   f He's a doctor.

7 The words in bold are incorrect. Write the correct words.

1 A: **Who** does he want a new car?   *Why*
    B: His car is very old.
2 A: **What** does your brother work?   ....
    B: In a coffee shop.
3 A: **What** does she come to university? ....
    B: She takes the bus.
4 A: **How** time does she go to work?   ....
    B: Nine o'clock.
5 A: **Where** does your sister do?   ....
    B: She's a nurse.
6 A: **How** does she go on holiday with? ....
    B: Her husband and children.

8 Look at the answers and write the questions. Use the question words in the box and the verbs in brackets.

How long	What	When	Where (x2)

1 A: *How long does the bus take?*   (take)
    B: The bus takes fifty minutes.
2 A: ....? (do)
    B: My brother's a bus driver.
3 A: ....? (work)
    B: Steven works in a school.
4 A: .... to the gym? (go)
    B: She goes to the gym on Fridays.
5 A: .... at two o'clock? (go)
    B: He goes to the park at two o'clock.

READING

9 Read the four texts. Who likes the things in his / her life? Tick (✓) the people.

Lucia [ ]   Ahmed [ ]   Greta [ ]   Vincenzo [ ]

Language note

A year is 365 days. There are 12 *months* in a year.

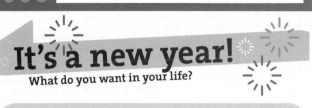

It's a new year!
What do you want in your life?

LUCIA   11:05, 1 JANUARY
I work for six days a week. I'm a doctor. I have a lot of money, but I don't have a lot of free time. That's OK. Money's important to me. My life is great. I don't want anything else!

AHMED   13:20, 1 JANUARY
I'm a nurse. I live in a bad area of the city. I like houses, but I don't like flats. I want a house – a big house in a good area of the city. I want to have a family. I want a lot of children. But it's very difficult.

GRETA   13:30, 1 JANUARY
It's my birthday this month (28th), but I don't want a party – I don't like them. But I want some things. I want $50 and a new phone. I don't like my phone. It's old!

VINCENZO   14:16, 1 JANUARY
I have a great job. I only work for three days a week. My wife works in a big office in the city. I have a son and a daughter. We are all well. We go on holidays to nice places. I like all the things in my life.

10 Read the questions. Circle the correct words.

1 (Does) / When Lucia work a lot?
2 Who / What is Lucia's job?
3 Where / What time does Ahmed live?
4 Does / What Ahmed live in a house or a flat?
5 Does / When Greta like birthday parties?
6 How much / Who money does Greta want for her birthday?
7 Why / Is Vincenzo married?
8 What / Does Vincenzo have children?

11 Tick (✓) the correct answers for the questions in Exercise 10.

1 a Yes.   [✓]   b No.   [ ]
2 a She's a teacher. [ ]   b She's a doctor.   [ ]
3 a In a bad area.   [ ]   b In a good area   [ ]
4 a A house.   [ ]   b A flat.   [ ]
5 a Yes.   [ ]   b No.   [ ]
6 a $28.   [ ]   b $50.   [ ]
7 a Yes.   [ ]   b No.   [ ]
8 a Yes.   [ ]   b No.   [ ]

VOCABULARY Things

1 Look at the pictures and complete the crossword.

Across →

2

4

6

7    8

Down ↓

1   3    5

2 Circle the word that is different in each group.

1 towel	soap	(map)
2 toothbrush	pen	toothpaste
3 money	dictionary	book
4 brush	mobile	charger
5 coat	clothes	food

DEVELOPING CONVERSATIONS
Asking for help in conversation

3 Complete the conversation with the words in the box.

again	Can	English	How	say	~~Sorry~~

Emma: Where are you from, Bandile?
Bandile: Buenos Aires.
Emma: [1] *Sorry*? Can you [2] .... that again?
Bandile: Buenos Aires, in Argentina.
Emma: Great. Welcome to London! Are you tired?
Bandile: Sorry. [3] .... you say that [4] ....?
Emma: Are you tired?
Bandile: Er ... yes. I'm hot and tired. I need to take a shower.
Emma: Oh, yes. Of course. Do you want anything?
Bandile: Do you have ... er, ... for my shower ...
Emma: A towel?
Bandile: No, I have a towel. I need some ... er, *seep*.
[5] .... do you say *seep* in [6] ....?
Emma: Soap!

4 🔊 **3.3 Listen and check your answers.**

GRAMMAR *a* and *any*

5 Write the words and phrases in the box in the correct column.

~~bags~~		book	brush	coat	food
local money		map	mobile	other shoes	toothpaste

Do you have a ...?	Do you have any ...?
....	*bags*
....	....
....	....
....	....
....	....

6 Choose the correct answers.

1 I don't have *a / any* other soap.
2 I don't need *a / anything* else.
3 Do you need *a / any* milk?
4 Do you want *a / anything*?
5 I don't have *a / any* pen.
6 Do you have *a / any* flat?
7 Do you have *a / any* maps?
8 I don't want *a / any* water.
9 Do you need *a / any* toothpaste?
10 Do you want *a / any* other drinks?
11 I don't want *a / any* money.

7 Complete the sentences so they are true for you. Write two or three things for each sentence. Use the words in the box or your own ideas.

big	expensive	good	new	old
car	clothes	flat	food	house
job	mobile	shoes		

1 I don't have ....
2 I don't want ....
3 I don't need ....

DEVELOPING WRITING
Writing an email

8 Read the email and tick (✓) the correct answers.
  1 Ismini is Sian's
    a teacher.   [ ]
    b friend.   [ ]
  2 The email is about
    a Ismini's life.   [ ]
    b Ismini's things. [ ]

```
● ● ●
┌─────────────────────────────────────────┐
│ Sent │ Chat │ Attach │ Font │            │
├─────────────────────────────────────────┤
│ Hi Sian,                                 │
│ Thanks for your email. I like my new job │
│ – it's great. I don't like the city! My  │
│ new school's not near my flat. I go by   │
│ bus and it takes me an hour. At the end  │
│ of the day, I'm very tired. I want to    │
│ work in a school near my flat. I want to │
│ walk to work and have more free time.    │
│ But it's very difficult. I need more     │
│ money!                                   │
│ Love,                                    │
│ Ismini                                   │
└─────────────────────────────────────────┘
```

9 Read the email again. Match (1–7) with (a–g).
  1 Ismini likes   [b]   a an hour.
  2 Ismini doesn't like   [   ]   b her new job.
  3 Ismini goes   [   ]   c more free time.
  4 The bus takes   [   ]   d the city.
  5 Ismini wants   [   ]   e more money.
  6 Ismini wants to   [   ]   f to her job by bus.
  7 Ismini needs   [   ]   g work in a school near
                                        her flat.

10 Write an email to a friend about your life. Write about things you have, things you want and things you don't want. Say why. Use the email in Exercise 8 to help you.

Vocabulary Builder Quiz 3

Download the Vocabulary Builder for Unit 3 and try the quiz below. Write your answers in your notebook. Then check them and record your score.

1 Circle the correct words.
  1 **read** *a book / only*
  2 **buy** *brush / clothes*
  3 **go** *shopping / work*
  4 **have** *a shower / weather*
  5 **get** *by train / married*
  6 **go on** *holiday / university*

2 Write the words in the box in the correct place.

charger	paste	phone	room	time (x2)

  1 hotel   ....
  2 free   ....
  3 mobile   ....
  4 tooth   ....
  5 phone   ....
  6 a long   ....

3 Complete the words in the sentences with the vowels (*a, e, i, o, u*).
  1 It's v__ry hot! It's 32°C!
  2 I need a sandwich. I'm h__ngry.
  3 English is d__ff__c__lt, but I like it.
  4 Do you have any __th__r paper?
  5 Do you like the l__c__l food?
  6 This is an __xp__ns__v__ charger. It's $50!
  7 *Bad, new* and *happy* are __dj__ct__v__s.

4 Match the beginnings (1–6) with the endings (a–f).
  1 I'm cold and   a a pen.
  2 I like local   b tired.
  3 I need soap and   c well.
  4 Her home is old and   d a towel.
  5 I'm not good. I'm not   e food.
  6 I want to write your   f small.
     phone number. I need

Score ____/25

Wait a couple of weeks and try the quiz again. Compare your scores.

04 WHERE AND WHEN?

VOCABULARY Places

1 Write the words in the box in the correct place.

machine	market	park	~~pool~~	shop	station

1 swimming *pool*
2 cash ....
3 train ....
4 car ....
5 super......................................
6 clothes ....

2 Complete the words with the vowels (*a, e, i, o, u*).

1 ch *u* rch
2 c __ f __
3 h __ sp __ t __ l
4 r __ st __ __ r __ nt
5 p __ rk

6 b __ nk
7 c __ n __ m __
8 h __ t __ l
9 m __ rk __ t

3 Label the photos with words from Exercises 1 and 2.

1 *church*

2 ....

3 ....

4 ....

5 ....

6 ....

7 ....

8 ....

9 ....

10 ....

GRAMMAR *Is there ... ? / There's ...*

4 Circle the correct words.

1 (*Is there*) / *There's* a train station near here?
2 *There's / Is there* a gym next to my office.
3 No, *there's / there isn't* a cash machine on this road, but there is a bank.
4 *Is there / There's* a swimming pool in the park.
5 No, *there isn't / there's* a bank near here. There's one in town.
6 *Is there / There's* a church in your village?
7 *There isn't / There's* a good clothes shop on this road, but it's expensive.
8 *There isn't / Is there* a market in this town?

5 Complete the conversation with *Is there, there's* and *there isn't.*

A: ¹ *Is there* a restaurant near here?
B: No, ² ....
A: OK. ³ ...., a café? I'm very hungry!
B: No, sorry, ⁴ .... one on this road.
A: Oh. ⁵ .... a supermarket?
B: Yes, ⁶ .... one next to the cinema! They have sandwiches.

6 ◔ 4.1 Listen and check your answers.

VOCABULARY EXTRA
Prepositions and directions

7 **Circle the correct words to label the pictures.**

1 (on) / in

2 on / next to

3 on the left / in

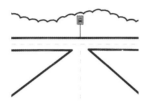

4 at the end / near

5 near / on

6 in / on the corner

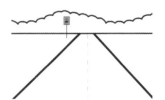

7 at / down the road

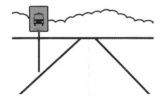

8 on the right / on the left

8 **Complete the sentences with the words in the box.**

at	~~down~~	in	near	next	on (x2)	right

1 Take the first road *down* here on the left.
2 The cash machine is .... to the café.
3 The café is .... here – it isn't far.
4 The car park is .... this road.
5 The hotel has a swimming pool – it's .... the hotel.
6 My house is .... the end of this road.
7 The supermarket is .... the corner.
8 The bank is down this road, on the ....

DEVELOPING CONVERSATIONS *called*

9 🔊 **4.2 Complete the sentences with the words in the box. Then listen and check.**

café	cinema	clothes shop	restaurant	town

1 A: Do you know a ***town*** called Southsea?
   B: No, is it far?
2 On Park Road, there's a .... called Nice and New. I often go shopping there.
3 There's a nice .... called Angelo's near my house. It has great pizza!
4 A: There's a .... called the Odeon there.
   B: Yes, do you want to see a film?
5 A: Do you know a .... called The CoffeeShop?
   B: Yes, it's very expensive.

LISTENING

10 🔊 **4.3 Listen to three conversations about places. Match the pictures (a–c) with the conversations (1–3).**

a

c

b

11 🔊 **4.3 Match the sentence beginnings (1–6) to their endings (a–f). Then listen and check.**

1 Do you know a café   *e*
2 There are some cafés near here,
3 No, there isn't a cash machine,
4 The bank is on
5 It's near a hospital
6 St Ann's is on the corner, on the right,
a and the swimming pool is on the left.
b but there's a bank on Maple Road.
c called St Ann's.
d but I don't know their names.
e called the Big Cappuccino on this road?
f the right.

PRONUNCIATION Syllable stress

> ### Language note
>
> A *syllable* is a part of a word that has a vowel sound
> (*a, e, i, o, u*).
> The word *park* has one syllable.
> The word *café* has two syllables: ca-fé.
> The word *cinema* has three syllables: ci-ne-ma.

1 🔊 **4.4 Listen to these words and tick (✓) the number of syllables in each word.**

1	bank	1 syllable [✓]	2 syllables [ ]
2	station	1 syllable [ ]	2 syllables [ ]
3	hospital	2 syllables [ ]	3 syllables [ ]
4	market	1 syllable [ ]	2 syllables [ ]
5	supermarket	3 syllables [ ]	4 syllables [ ]
6	church	1 syllable [ ]	2 syllables [ ]

> ### Language note
>
> We often stress one syllable in a word, e.g. **doc**tor,
> **tea**cher, **fath**er

2 🔊 **4.5 Listen to four words. Underline the stressed syllable.**
1 station
2 hospital
3 market
4 supermarket

VOCABULARY Days and times of day

3 Write the days of the week in the correct order.

Friday	Monday	Saturday	~~Sunday~~	Thursday
Tuesday	Wednesday			

1 *Sunday*
2 ....
3 ....
4 ....
5 ....
6 ....
7 ....

4 Circle the word that is different in each group.

1	today	tomorrow	(night)
2	yesterday	afternoon	tomorrow
3	evening	yesterday	morning
4	morning	night	today
5	afternoon	evening	tomorrow

5 Complete the text with the words in the box.

afternoon	evening	from	morning	night	to

I get to work in the ¹ .... at 8. I have lunch at 1. Then
I work ² .... 2 in the ³ .... to 6. In the ⁴ ....
I get to my house at 7 and I am very tired. At ⁵ ....
I usually sleep from 11 ⁶ .... 6.30.

6 Complete the groups with the correct days.

Friday	Monday	Saturday	~~Thursday~~
Tuesday	Wednesday		

1 Today: Wednesday   Tomorrow: *Thursday*
  Yesterday: ....
2 Today: ....   Tomorrow: Sunday
  Yesterday: ....
3 Today: Tuesday   Tomorrow: ....
  Yesterday: ....

GRAMMAR
Adverbs of frequency

7 Write the words in the box in the correct place.

always	~~never~~	normally	sometimes	usually

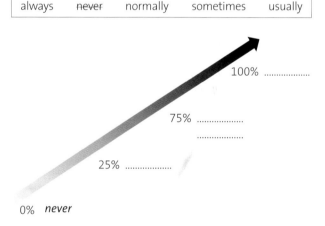

100% ....
75% ....
....
25% ....
0% *never*

8 Complete the sentences with adverbs of frequency.
1 You *always* go shopping on Saturday morning.   (100%)
2 We .... go swimming in
  the evening.   (25%)
3 She .... walks to her office.   (0%)
4 He .... takes the train to the
  city centre.   (75%)
5 They .... go to Mexico on holiday.   (65%)

9 Complete the sentences so that they are true for you.
1 I always .... in the morning.
2 I usually .... in the afternoon.
3 I sometimes .... in the evening.
4 I never .... on Saturday.
5 I normally .... on Sunday.

READING

10 Read the article and tick (✓) the best title.

a   The Working Week   [   ]
b   My Weekend   [   ]
c   Shops in Canada   [   ]

---

by Janet Ferguson

I'm from Nova Scotia, Canada. It's a great place.

In Nova Scotia, people usually work 40 hours a week. Lots of people have Sunday free. I'm a teacher and I work in a school in a small village. I always have Saturday and Sunday free.

On Saturday, I usually take the bus to the city. I sometimes go to a supermarket called Sobey's and I sometimes go to a clothes shop called Winners.

On Sunday, I normally go to the market in my village. It always opens at 10 in the morning and closes at 4 in the afternoon. I always buy fresh fruit at the market. I meet friends at our favourite café in the evening.

I like my job, but I love weekends!

---

11 Circle the correct words.

1   People in Nova Scotia *always* / *usually* work 40 hours a week.
2   Janet *never* / *always* has Sunday free.
3   Janet *normally* / *sometimes* takes the bus to the city.
4   The market in Janet's village is *always* / *never* open in the morning on Sunday.

12 Answer the questions.

1   Where is Janet from? *She's from Nova Scotia, Canada.*
2   What is Janet's job?
   ....
3   Where does Janet work?
   ....
4   Where does Janet go shopping on Saturday?
   ....
5   What time does the market close on Sunday?
   ....
6   What does Janet always buy on Sunday?
   ....
7   Who does Janet meet on Sunday evening?
   ....
8   What does Janet like?
   ....
9   What does Janet love?
   ....

13 Now read the article again and check.

Learner tip

Read, read, read! Reading is a very good way to learn more English. You see and learn more words. Try reading these in English:
– free newspapers and magazines
– news on the internet
– websites about things you are interested in
– books for children or young adults

GRAMMAR *Can ...?*

1 🔊 **4.6 Listen and number the questions in the order you hear them.**

a Can you close the window?   [   ]
b Can you do Exercises 4 and 5?   [   ]
c Can we have food in the class?   [   ]
d Can you wait ten minutes?   [   ]
e Can we have a break?   [   ]
f Can you help me?   [   ]

2 Complete the questions with *Can I* or *Can you*.

1 I'm tired. ***Can I*** have a break?
2 This is difficult. .... help me?
3 .... do Exercises 4 and 5 for homework, please?
4 I don't have time to eat my sandwich. .... have five more minutes?
5 .... wait two minutes? I need to go to the toilet.
6 .... have my coffee in the class?

3 Write questions.

1 We can have a break.
   Can we have a break?
2 We can have ten more minutes.
   ....
3 We can't have food in the class.
   ....
4 You can close the window.
   ....
5 You can do Exercise 9.
   ....
6 You can help me.
   ....
7 You can wait a minute.
   ....

VOCABULARY Classroom verbs

4 Match the verbs 1–8 with a–h.

1 come   [*c*]   a the light
2 leave   [   ]   b at the front
3 play   [   ]   c in
4 share   [   ]   d your tablet
5 sit   [   ]   e it again
6 turn on   [   ]   f early
7 use   [   ]   g it on the board
8 write   [   ]   h your book

5 Complete the conversations with words from Exercise 4.

1 A: Can we have a break?
   B: No, but you can *leave* early.
2 A: I can't see my book!
   B: .... the light.
3 A: I'm late. Sorry.
   B: That's OK. .... in.
4 A: I don't understand. Can you .... it on the board?
   B: Sure.
5 A: I don't know this word.
   B: .... your tablet.
6 A: I don't have my book. Can you ....
   your book?
   B: OK.

DEVELOPING WRITING
A note describing where you live

Language note

When you write in English, you can use words like *and* and *but* to make two short sentences one long sentence.
There's a church. There's a school. = *There's a church **and** a school.*
There's a bus station. There isn't a train station. = *There's a bus station, **but** there isn't a train station.*

6 Complete the sentences with *and* or *but*.

1 I work late on Monday, ... I don't work on Tuesday.
2 There's a cash machine here, ... there isn't a bank.
3 I have a pen .... I have paper.
4 There's a park .... there's a supermarket.
5 My sister lives in a village, ... I live in a big town.
6 Jo goes to the café on Saturday morning .... meets her friends.

7 Read the note quickly and circle the correct answer.

1 Marcia's note is for:
   a her doctor
   b her father
   c her friend
2 The note is about:
   a work
   b places
   c school

Hi Juan,

Sorry I'm not here, but this is my flat – Flat 12,
¹ **20 Garden Road**! This is a nice area and I love it!
There's a café on the corner and a restaurant next to
the flat. There isn't a museum here, but you can
² .... to the centre. There's a
³ .... The City Museum. It normally
opens ⁴ .... and it usually closes at 7 at
night. It's always closed on Monday. There's a clothes shop
⁵ ...., but I always go shopping in the
centre. There are lots of good clothes shops there.
Have a great holiday!

Marcia

8 **Complete Marcia's note to Juan with the phrases in the box.**

~~20 Garden Road~~	at 10 in the morning
down the road	museum there called
take the train	

9 **Complete the notes for your home.**
This is my house/flat – ....
There's ....
It normally opens at .... and it usually closes
at ....
It's always closed on ....
There isn't ....
You can take the .... to ....

10 **Write a note for a friend who is going to stay in your home. Use your notes from Exercise 9. Use the model text in Exercise 7.**

Vocabulary Builder Quiz 4

Download the Vocabulary Builder for Unit 4 and try the quiz below. Write your answers in your notebook. Then check them and record your score.

1 **Circle the correct words.**
1 **see** *night / a film*
2 **need** *$5 / shopping*
3 **open** *a shop / a light*
4 **study** *a market / English*
5 **share** *your homework / your tablet*

2 **Write the words in the box in the correct place.**

machine	name	park	shop	station

1 cash ....
2 train ....
3 clothes ....
4 car ....
5 family ....

3 **Match the beginnings (1–5) with the endings (a–e).**
1 What time do you get   a off the TV, please?
2 The school is next   b up every day?
3 Can you turn   c at the front of the room?
4 Is the teacher   d to the park.
5 Sorry, I'm late. Can I come   e in, please?

4 **Complete the groups with the words in the box.**

book	evening	mosque	third	today

1 first   second   ....
2 church   religion   ....
3 morning   afternoon   ....
4 board   classroom   ....
5 yesterday   tomorrow   ....

5 **Complete the words in the sentences.**
1 How m..................... supermarkets are in this area?
2 The cinema is on the left and the bank is on the r.....................
3 Do you know a restaurant c..................... D'Angelos?
4 Oh, no! The supermarket is c.....................! I need milk and bread!
5 A: I don't u..................... this word.
   B: Use your dictionary.

Score ___/25

Wait a couple of weeks and try the quiz again.
Compare your scores.

VOCABULARY Getting there

1 Complete the table with the words in the box. Sometimes more than one answer is correct.

a taxi	for the bus	home	off the train
the metro	the red line	to work	trains

get	go	take
a taxi		
walk	**change**	**wait**

2 Complete the conversations with verbs from Exercise 1.

1 A: I work in an office on Scotland Road.
   B: How do you get there?
   A: I usually *get* a taxi or I sometimes .... on nice days.

2 A: Can you help me, please? I want to go to the main square.
   B: OK. .... the blue line and .... trains at Central Station.

3 A: I don't feel very well.
   B: Do you want to .... home? You can leave early.

4 A: I usually .... about ten minutes for the bus to school.
   B: Oh. I always .... the metro.

5 A: To get to my flat, ... off the train at Sloan Station.
   B: Can you say that again?
   A: Yes, Sloan Station.

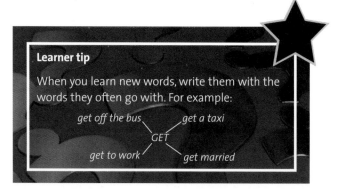

Learner tip

When you learn new words, write them with the words they often go with. For example:

get off the bus   get a taxi
            GET
get to work   get married

GRAMMAR Are there ... ? / There are ...

3 Choose the correct option (a, b or c).

A: Do you like my new flat, Jason?
B: Yes, it's great! [1] .... any interesting places near here?
A: Yes, [2] .... lots of good places. You like museums. [3] .... two interesting museums in this area.
B: Cool! And I want to go shopping. Are there [4] .... shops near here?
A: No, [5] .... shops, but [6] .... a great market in the Old Town.
B: [7] .... a café in the Old Town?
A: Yes, there's [8] .... café called Coffee Express. It's really nice. Do you want to go there?
B: Yes, I need a coffee!

1	a Is there	b There are	ⓒ Are there
2	a there are	b there's	c is there
3	a There's	b There are	c There aren't
4	a a	b some	c any
5	a there isn't	b there are no	c there are
6	a there's	b there are	c are there
7	a there's	b Is there	c Are there
8	a some	b a	c any

4 🔊 5.1 Listen and check your answers.

5 Correct the <u>underlined mistakes</u> in the sentences.

1 I'm hungry. ~~There are~~ any nice restaurants near here?
   Are there

2 I need some new clothes for the party. Is there <u>some</u> good clothes shop near here? ....

3 <u>There are</u> a new supermarket in my area. I want to go shopping there! ....

4 We want a coffee and a sandwich. <u>There is no</u> café on this road? ....

5 <u>There's</u> three or four interesting places in the Old Town. ....

6 I want to go on holiday in Barcelona. Are there a good hotels there? ....

6 Write sentences about where you live.

1 There's ....
2 There are ....
3 There isn't a ....

7 Write questions to ask a friend about where they live.

1 Is there a .... ?
2 Are there any .... ?

DEVELOPING CONVERSATIONS *best*

8 Write *best* in the correct place.

          best
1 It's far from here. It's ʌto take a taxi.

2 Where's the place to see some interesting art?

3 What's the area in the city?

4 Is that the café to sit and have a coffee?

5 Where's the place to go swimming?

LISTENING

9 🔊 **5.2 Listen to five conversations. Where do the
people want to go? Match the photos (a–e) with
the conversations (1–5).**

Conversation 1	photo [*b*]
Conversation 2	photo [ ]
Conversation 3	photo [ ]
Conversation 4	photo [ ]
Conversation 5	photo [ ]

10 🔊 **5.2 Listen again. Are the sentences true or false?
Circle T or F.**

1	There's a restaurant on North Road.	(T)	F
2	There are some good cafés on North Road.	T	F
3	The market is in the city centre.	T	F
4	The supermarket is forty minutes from the village.	T	F
5	The cash machine is near the bank.	T	F
6	The cash machine is near a hospital.	T	F
7	The museum is called the City Museum.	T	F
8	There are fifteen museums on Gosposka Street.	T	F
9	The Old Square is a good place to have a walk.	T	F
10	There are no nice places near the Old Square.	T	F

VOCABULARY Buying tickets

1 Complete the phrases with the vowels (a, e, i, o, u).
1 ch a ng e tr a i ns
2 p __ y by c __ rd
3 f __ rst cl __ ss
4 the n __ xt tr __ __ n
5 r __ t __ rn
6 s __ c __ nd cl __ ss
7 s __ ngl __

2 Look at the photos and complete the crossword.

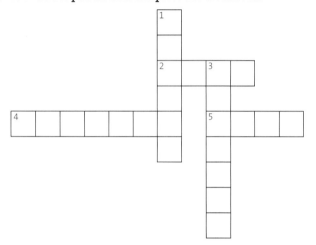

Across →
2 4 5

Down ↓
1 3

3 Circle the correct words.
1 Excuse me. Can you help me? Where do I enter / *change*
  trains for Covent Garden?
2 You can *buy* / *pay* by cash or *card* / *ticket*.
3 The best way to go is *first class* / *second class*, but it's
  expensive.
4 I need a bus ticket. Can I use that *cash* / *machine*?
5 Put your card in here and *enter* / *pay* your number.
6 I need a ticket, please – a *return* / *single*. I'm back
  tomorrow.
7 Hello there. Is the *next* / *single* train at 9.32?
8 Thank you. And here is your *receipt* / *machine*.

PRONUNCIATION /k/ and /s/

**4 Read these words and think about the sound of the
letters in bold. What are the two different sounds?**

card	**c**ash	**c**entre	**c**ity
costs	first **c**lass	offi**c**e	re**c**eipt

5 ✪ 5.3 Listen and write the words.

/k/	/s/
card	....
....	....
....	....
....	....

Language note

The letter *c* has the sound /k/ before a consonant or
vowels *a, o* and *u*, but /s/ before vowels *e, i, y*.

6 ✪ 5.3 Listen again and repeat.

READING

**7 Read the three adverts for bus trips. Which advert talks
about how many people you travel with? Tick (✓) the
correct answer.**

Advert 1   [ ]
Advert 2   [ ]
Advert 3   [ ]

8 Circle the correct answers.
Advert 1
1 ⓐ You can visit nine other places.
  b You can visit twelve other places.
2 a A return costs £1,230.
  b A single costs $1,640.
Advert 2
3 a You sleep on the bus.
  b You sleep in hotels.
4 a There are twelve passengers on the bus.
  b There are fifteen passengers on the bus.
Advert 3
5 a You travel only to Lima.
  b You travel to Lima and Cusco.
6 a You can get off the bus.
  b You can't get off the bus.

9 Now read the adverts again and check.

FIRST CLASS TRIPS
Buses are cheap and they are the best! Take the bus!

❶ **Take the bus** from London and visit nine different cities in Europe. Sleep in great hotels and eat in the best restaurants! The trip takes twelve days and a return ticket costs £1,230 ($1,640). You can sit and see the world outside. You can get great views from the bus. You can see Paris, and the beautiful mountains in Switzerland and Italy.

❷ **Take the bus** from Helsinki to Berlin. The journey takes five days. You sleep in hotels and you can get off and visit lots of interesting places. There are only twelve passengers on the bus. You can sit and talk together. It only costs $450!

❸ **Take the bus** and see Peru in South America. Have a walk down the streets of Lima. Sit and have a coffee in the afternoon or have dinner in the evening in the main square of Cusco. The trip takes eight days. That's a lot of time to make friends! It costs £2,095. Have a great trip!

DEVELOPING CONVERSATIONS
Where are you going?

10 ⬤ 5.4 **Where are the people going? Listen and match the conversations (1–5) to the places (a–e).**

Conversation 1	[d]	a	to Cannes
Conversation 2	[ ]	b	to the main square
Conversation 3	[ ]	c	to Berlin
Conversation 4	[ ]	d	to Truro
Conversation 5	[ ]	e	to the Old Town

GRAMMAR
Talking about plans: *I'm* / *We're going*

1 Look at the <u>underlined</u> words in the sentences. Write them in the correct column in the table.

Where	What	When
to the bank		

1 We're going <u>to the bank</u> after the class.
2 I'm going <u>to the market</u> this afternoon.
3 I'm going to have dinner with Lucy <u>this evening</u>.
4 We're going to meet friends <u>now</u>.
5 I'm going <u>to see some interesting art</u> tonight.
6 We're going <u>to the museum</u> tomorrow.
7 We're going <u>to go swimming</u> on Sunday.
8 I'm going <u>home</u> at five.

2 Complete the sentences with *'m going* or *'re going*.
1 I *'m going* to play football at five.
2 Dom and I – we .... to the supermarket on Saturday.
3 We .... to have a walk after work.
4 I .... to the park this afternoon.
5 I .... to bed now.
6 We .... to see a film tomorrow.

3 Complete the sentences with *'m going to* or *'re going to* and a verb from the box.

eat	have	meet	play	see	stay

1 I .... football this afternoon with some friends.
2 We .... a coffee after the class.
3 I .... my sister in town tomorrow.
4 Do you want to come to the cinema? We .... *Ocean's 8*.
5 I'm hungry. I .... my sandwich.
6 We .... at home and watch a film tonight.

4 Complete the sentences for you.
1 Tonight I ....
2 Tomorrow I ....
3 At the weekend I ....
4 Next week I ....

GRAMMAR
Asking about plans: *going* and *doing*

5 Complete the sentences with *going* or *doing*.
1 Where are you *going*?
2 Are you .... to the café?
3 What are you .... this evening?
4 What time are you ....?
5 What are you .... on Monday?

6 Complete the conversations with the questions in the box.

Are you going	What are you doing
What time are you going	Where are you going

1 A: I'm going to go shopping at two.
  B: .... ?
  A: The clothes shop on Bayer's Road.
2 A: I'm going to London on Sunday. Do you want to come?
  B: .... ?
  A: Nine or ten in the morning.
3 A: Are you going to the gym tonight?
  B: Yes. .... , too?
  A: Yes. Do you want to share a taxi?
4 A: .... after the class?
  B: I'm going to the cinema. Do you want to come?
  A: Sorry. I can't. I'm going to stay here.

DEVELOPING WRITING
Writing a text message

Language note
- -

Nouns are words like *ticket*, *Marie* and *Tom*.
Pronouns are words like *it*, *she*, *he* and *they*.
When you write, try not to use the same nouns again and again – use pronouns.
Here's your ticket. ~~Your ticket~~ It is a single.
I'm going to meet Tom. ~~Tom~~ He is my brother.

7 Circle the correct option.
1 I'm going to the gym with Karim. *He / It* works in my office.
2 There's a ticket machine in the train station. *It's / She's* next to platform 5.
3 I'm going to go shopping with Lily. *It's / She's* my friend.
4 I'm going to the museum with Brad and Lee. *He / They* are my brothers.

8 Complete the sentences with the pronouns in the box.

He	It	She	They

1 I'm going on holiday with Jane. ....'s my sister.
2 I'm going to sit and have lunch with Sebastian. ....'s my son.
3 I'm going to share a taxi with Bridget and Liam. .... are married.
4 There's a bank on this street. ....'s on the corner.

9 Read the text quickly. What is it?
a a blog   b a text message   c a letter

Hi, Lydia. What are you doing [1] **tonight**? I'm going to
[2] .... in town with my friend, Karim.
We're going to see [3] .... – it's a great
film. Do you want to come? To get to the cinema,
take [4] .... It's the blue line. Get off at
Victoria Station. I'll meet you outside the cinema at
[5] ....

10 Now complete the text with the phrases in the box.

Deadpool 2	eight	the cinema
the metro	tonight	

11 Make plans to do something with a friend. Complete the notes.
I'm going to .... (what?) ....
(where?) .... (when?).
I'm going with .... (who?).
To get to .... (what?), take ....
(how?)
Get off .... (where?).
I'll meet you .... (where?) at ....
(what time?).

12 Write a text message to a friend. Use your notes from Exercise 11. Use the model text in Exercise 9.

Vocabulary Builder Quiz 5

Download the Vocabulary Builder for Unit 5 and try the quiz below. Write your answers in your notebook. Then check them and record your score.

1 Circle the correct words.
1 I'm going to the cinema at three *later / o'clock*.
2 You can see the world *outside / there* on a bus trip.
3 Can I pay by *receipt / cash*?
4 There are some cafés in the *cheap / main* square.
5 How many *passengers / parties* are going to Liverpool?

2 Put the letters in the correct order and write the words.
1 How long is your (liftgh) .... to Rome?
2 Take the red (neil) .... and change at Victoria station.
3 Can I have a (tunrer) ...., please? I'm back on Monday.
4 We had a good holiday in Australia, but it was a long (ojneyur) ....
5 We're going to see a lot of beautiful (wsvei) .... on our holiday.

3 Circle the incorrect words.

1 **sleep**	well	every	at night
2 **get off**	second class	at the park	the train
3 **get**	to my house	here	a long time
4 **talk**	work	about a trip	to friends
5 **put**	your bag there	money in the machine	some help

4 Complete the sentences with the words in the box.

card	football	home	museum	platform

1 I'm sorry, but I want to stay at .... tonight.
2 I want to buy a ticket. Can I pay by ....?
3 Do you want to play .... next weekend?
4 I'm going to visit a .... in the Old Town.
5 A: We're going to Leeds.
   B: OK. Wait on .... 12.

5 Match the beginnings (1–5) with the endings (a–e).
1 Don't take a bus. You can take
2 It's the break. Are you going to eat
3 A ticket to Southsea costs
4 Please enter
5 Do you want to share

a £10.
b your number here.
c a sandwich?
d the metro.
e a taxi to the airport?

Score ____ /25

Wait a couple of weeks and try the quiz again.
Compare your scores.

VOCABULARY Problems

1 Label the photos. Put the letters in the correct order and write the words.

1 eatl *late*

2 nseoi ....

3 inra ....

4 on-neo ....

5 retid ....

6 ffictra ....

2 Circle the correct word.

1 A: Is that Jane's flat?
   B: No, we're in the right area, but we're in the *wrong* / *tired* road!

2 A: There's a lot of *noise* / *traffic* today.
   B: Yes, and it's all going to the city centre!

3 A: What's that *problem* / *noise* outside our room?
   B: I don't know, but I can't sleep.

4 A: Is there a lot of *rain* / *traffic* in London?
   B: Yes, and I don't like it. I like hot weather.

5 A: We need to buy our train tickets.
   B: Yes, but there's *nowhere* / *no-one* here to help us.

6 A: Are you *tired* / *late*, Stephan?
   B: Yes, I want to go to bed.

7 A: We're going to the cinema this evening. Do you want to come?
   B: Sorry, I need to work *wrong* / *late*.

8 A: The train is very busy.
   B: Yes, and there's *no-one* / *nowhere* to sit.

9 A: I have *a problem* / *rain* at the office.
   B: Oh, do you need to work this evening?

> **Learner tip**
>
> Write different sentences with the new words you learn, or practise using new words in conversation with a classmate or another English speaker/ learner. You need to use a new word about ten to fifteen times before you remember it.

GRAMMAR Past simple: irregular verbs

3 Complete the table with the past simple form of the verbs.

Present simple	Past simple
(be) is	1 *was*
(be) are	2
have / has	3
go / goes	4
do / does	5

4 Complete the sentences with the verbs in brackets. Use the past simple.

1 We *were* (be) late for the party yesterday.

2 I'm tired. I .... (have) a lot of problems at the office today.

3 My friends .... (go) to China on their last holiday.

4 Sorry, I'm late. There .... (be) a lot of traffic.

5 It .... (be) a great trip! We .... (do) a lot of things and we .... (go) to a lot of interesting places.

6 I .... (be) wrong about the flight number last week. Sorry!

7 I .... (do) a lot of work this morning.

DEVELOPING CONVERSATIONS

Don't worry / That's OK

5 ✿ **6.1 Complete the conversations with the words in the box. Listen and check your answers.**

Don't	OK	~~That~~	That's	worry

1 A: Hi, Maria. Sorry, I'm late.
   B: *That*'s OK. How was your journey?
2 A: I don't have any money for lunch.
   B: .... worry. I have some.
3 A: Sorry, I'm late. I went to the wrong flat.
   B: That's .... You're here now!
4 A: I can't come to the cinema. I had a problem at home.
   B: Don't .... We can go tomorrow.
5 A: I don't have my English book.
   B: .... OK. You can share my book.

READING

6 Read the email quickly. Where did Berat and his brother go on holiday? Tick the correct answer.
a Ankara [ ]   b Barcelona [ ]   c Japan [ ]

7 Are the sentences true or false? Circle T or F.
1 The journey from Ankara to Barcelona was good, but it was long.   (T)   F
2 Berat and his brother were only on one plane.   T   F
3 Their room was expensive.   T   F
4 They did a lot of things on their holiday.   T   F
5 La Rambla had no noise or traffic.   T   F
6 It was hot, but there was rain.   T   F

8 Circle the correct words.
1 Berat and his brother are from *Spain /* (*Turkey.*)
2 Their journey was *six hours and thirty minutes / six hours and thirteen minutes.*
3 Their hotel was in *La Rambla / Via Laietana.*
4 *Via Laietana / La Rambla* had a lot of interesting places on it.
5 They went to a swimming pool near their hotel every *evening / morning.*

9 Now read the email again and check.

Sent   Chat   Attach   Font

Hi Siobhan,

How are you? My brother and I had a great trip to Spain. The journey from Ankara, in Turkey, to Barcelona was good, but it was long – six hours and thirty minutes. We changed planes in Munich, Germany.

Our hotel in the city was called Hotel Colonial Barcelona. It was in a busy street called Via Laietana. Our room was expensive – $103 for one night, but it was a good hotel in the best area of the city.

We did a lot of things on our holiday. We went to a road in the city centre called La Rambla. It had some interesting places on it. It had cafés, restaurants and places to go shopping. It was nice, but there was a lot of noise and traffic.

The weather was great. It was hot and there was no rain! We went to a swimming pool near our hotel every evening.

Well, it's late and I'm tired now. I want to go to bed! How was your holiday in Japan?

Write soon,
Berat

VOCABULARY Hotels and checking in

1 Circle the correct words to label the pictures.

1 (check out)/ booking

2 number / bag

3 lift / room

4 breakfast / passport

5 key / password

6 lift / booking

7 address / password

8 breakfast / passport

2 Complete the sentences with words from Exercise 1.
1 My *address* is 26 Seaview Road, Flat .... 4.
2 Do you have your .... ? You need it to get on the plane!
3 We want to have .... in the morning before we .... of the hotel.
4 Here's the .... for your room. It's room 258, on the second floor.
5 The .... is over there – you don't need to use the stairs.
6 We have a .... for two nights. My name is Ahmed Asfour.
7 We want to use the WiFi. What's the .... ?
8 Can you help me with my .... , please? It's very big!

GRAMMAR Regular past simple endings

Language note

Most regular verbs add *-ed* in the past simple.
*work > work**ed*** *want > want**ed***

Regular verbs that end in an *e* add *-d* in the past simple.
*liv**e** > live**d*** *us**e** > use**d***

3 Complete the table with the past simple form of the verbs in the box.

like	love	rain	share	stay	talk

verb + -*d*	verb + -*ed*
liked	

4 Complete the sentences with the verbs in brackets. Use the past simple.
1 We *liked* (like) the local food.
2 I .... (stay) in a five-star hotel in Belfast.
3 It .... (rain) every day on my holiday.
4 We .... (love) the café in our hostel in Cuba.
5 Mr Smith .... (talk) to my mother yesterday.
6 I .... (share) a room with my sister on holiday.

PRONUNCIATION Past simple forms

5 🔊 **6.2 Listen to these past simple forms. Do the letters in bold sound the same or different? Write the words in the correct column of the table.**

lik**ed**	rain**ed**	visit**ed**

/t/	/d/	/id/
liked		

6 🔊 **6.3 Listen to these past forms and write them in the correct column of the table in Exercise 5.**

danced	needed	shared	started	stayed
talked	walked	wanted	watched	

7 🔊 **6.3 Listen again and repeat.**

GRAMMAR Past simple negatives

8 Write the past negative form of the verbs.
1 had   *didn't have*
2 liked   ....
3 rained   ....
4 saw   ....
5 talked   ....
6 was   ....
7 went   ....
8 were   ....
9 did   ....

9 Make the sentences negative.
1 It rained in my city on Friday.
It didn't rain in my city on Friday.
2 On my trip, I saw interesting art.
....
3 At school, I talked to my English teacher.
....
4 I had a party last weekend.
....
5 On my holiday, I liked the local food.
....
6 I did a lot of work today.
....
7 On my bus journey, there was a lot of noise.
....
8 I went shopping yesterday.
....

10 Tick the sentences in Exercise 9 that are true for you.

LISTENING

11 🔊 **6.4 Listen to the conversation between Chang and his wife. Why is Chang late home from work? Tick (✓) the correct picture.**

1 ☐

2 ☐

3 ☐

12 Match the sentence beginnings (1–9) with the endings (a–i).

1 There was   [*f*]   a no-one to help me.
2 How was   [   ]   b work?
3 It wasn't   [   ]   c very big.
4 The shop was very busy,   d lunch this afternoon.
   but there was   [   ]   e to bed late last night.
5 Yes, I didn't have   [   ]   f a lot of traffic in the
6 I didn't like   [   ]   centre.
7 It wasn't   [   ]   g a lot of work today
8 I did   [   ]   and I'm tired.
9 I went   [   ]   h very good.
                     i that restaurant.

13 🔊 **6.4 Listen again and check your answers.**

GRAMMAR
Past simple questions

1 Circle the correct words.
1 What *did you have* / *did you had* for lunch today?
2 Where *went you* / *did you go* on holiday last year?
3 What time *did you leave* / *you did leave* for work/school this morning?
4 What films *were you saw* / *did you see* last week?
5 What time *did you get* / *did you got* to work/school this morning?
6 *Did you go* / *Went you* out last Saturday night?
7 What *did you* / *did you do* last weekend?
8 *Did you went* / *Did you go* shopping yesterday?

2 Write true answers to the questions in Exercise 1.

3 Complete the questions with *you* and the past simple form of the verbs in the box. Then match the questions (1–6) with the answers (a–f).

~~buy~~	get up	go	live	stay	study

1 What *did you buy* at the shops yesterday?
2 Where .... in 2015? A house or a flat?
3 Where .... last night?
4 What time .... this morning?
5 What........................... at university?
6 .... at home every day last week?

a   In a flat.   [   ]
b   No, only on Monday, Wednesday and Friday.   [   ]
c   Some clothes and a bag.   [*1*]
d   To the gym.   [   ]
e   At seven.   [   ]
f   English.   [   ]

GRAMMAR REVIEW: Past simple

4 Put the words in the correct order.
1 at the café / was / there / a problem
   There was a problem at the café.
2 for class / weren't / we / late
   ....
3 had / at home / I / breakfast
   ....
4 to the museum / didn't / they / go
   ....
5 a lot of / we / interesting things / did
   ....
6 ? / get / you / home / did / when
   ....
7 like / I / Rome / didn't
   ....

8 a great hostel / we / in / stayed
   ....
9 ? / you / the doctor / did / talk to
   ....
10 ? / you / did / dinner / where / have
   ....

5 Complete the conversations with the words in brackets. Use the correct past simple form.
1 A: Why are you late?
   B: Sorry. The weather *was* (be) very bad.
2 A: Why are you tired?
   B: I .... (go) to bed late last night.
3 A: What .... (you / have) for lunch?
   B: I .... (not have) lunch –
      I .... (be) very busy.
4 A: Where .... (you / stay) in Peru?
   B: We .... (stay) in Lima.
5 A: How .... (be) the restaurant?
   B: Good. There .... (not be) a lot of
      people there.
6 A: .... (you / like) the hostel?
   B: No, we .... (share) a bathroom with
      ten other people!
7 A: What .... (you / see) at the museum
      yesterday?
   B: We .... (not go) to the museum.
      We .... (walk) around the Old Town.

DEVELOPING WRITING
Writing a review

Language note
- -
When you write in English, always watch your spelling.
Some words sound the same, but have different spelling
and meaning.

*I went **to** Indonesia.*
*I saw **two** lakes.*

*I went **there** in December.*
*They had lunch with **their** mother.*

***We're** in our rooms.*
*The rooms **were** nice.*

6 Circle the correct words.
1 We went *to* / *two* South Africa on our holiday.
2 They did lots of things with *there* / *their* friends.
3 The views *were* / *we're* great.
4 We saw *to* / *two* markets in the Old Town.
5 *Were* / *We're* at the hostel.
6 I went *there* / *their* by plane.

7 **Read the review quickly and circle the correct answer.**
The review is for:
a a country b a holiday c a hotel

journeyadvice (Bali)

Tell us about your holiday in Bali. We're waiting for your reviews!

Bali Green Hostel
★ ★ ★ ★

I stayed in a hostel called the Bali Green Hostel for five days and I shared a room with six other people. The room cost $16 for one night. I went to the hostel very late at night, but that wasn't a problem. There was someone there – he worked all night. My room was very clean and my bed was new. There were towels and soap in the bathroom. The hostel didn't have a restaurant, but it had a café. The food and service were good and the café wasn't expensive. The hostel was near a supermarket and a beautiful beach. I did some interesting things in Bali. One day, I went on a trip to Kuta with some new friends. I saw a very old temple there. I had lunch at a nice restaurant and talked to lots of local people. Another day I went shopping at a market. I loved my holiday!

8 **Write a review of a holiday. Complete the notes.**
I went to .... on my holiday.
I stayed in a .... for .... days.
I didn't share / shared a .... with ....
The room cost .... for ....
My room was .... and ....
There were .... and .... in the ....
The .... didn't have ...., but it had ....
The .... was near .... and ....
One day, I went ....
Another day I ....

9 **Write a review of a holiday. Use your notes from Exercise 8 and the model review in Exercise 7. Remember to check your spelling.**

Vocabulary Builder Quiz 6

Download the Vocabulary Builder for Unit 6 and try the quiz below. Write your answers in your notebook. Then check them and record your score.

1 **Circle the correct words.**
1 I like modern *music / noise*. Katy Perry is my favourite singer.
2 It's late. There's *nowhere / no-one* in my office.
3 Great to see you! How was your *plane / flight*?
4 Hi, my room number is 12. Can I have the WiFi *password / address*, please?
5 Did you like your *tour / journey* of London?

2 **Complete the words in the sentences.**
1 Sorry, I'm late. There was a lot of t .... in the city.
2 I didn't have breakfast and now I'm really h ....
3 Hi, my name is Janet Dean. I have a b .... for two nights.
4 A: Do you like this song?
   B: Yes, that's my favourite b .... !
5 A: Here's our room. Oh, no! Where's our k .... ?
   B: It's OK. I have it in my bag.

3 **Circle the incorrect words.**

1	**a busy**	party	gym	city centre
2	**clean**	the bathroom	your bed	the car
3	**have**	dinner	lunch	exercise
4	**last**	weather	night	year
5	**a quiet**	time of day	problem	hostel

4 **Complete the sentences with the words in the box.**

lake	lift	passport	rain	star

1 I need a .... I'm going to China next year.
2 It's a five-..................................... hotel. It's expensive, but very nice.
3 Our hotel was near a .... We went swimming every day!
4 We get lots of .... in London.
5 Your room is on the third floor. You can use the .... over there.

5 **Match the beginnings (1–5) with the endings (a–e).**
1 How was your holiday? Did you stay
2 I'm very tired. I want to sleep
3 Hello, Mr Peters. Can you sign
4 Did you meet
5 I'm going to watch

a here, please?
b in a nice hotel?
c a film tonight.
d for one or two hours.
e any interesting people in Rome?

Score ____/25

Wait a couple of weeks and try the quiz again.
Compare your scores.

VOCABULARY Words for activities

1 Complete the table with the words in the box.

a football game	a magazine	a series on TV
Italian food	on the internet	running
shopping	some exercise	stories
to a band	to a song	to concerts
videos		

(a football game is crossed out)

cook	do	go

read	listen	watch
		a football game

2 Match the pictures (1–7) to the sentences (a–g).

 1 d

 2

 3

 4

 5

 6

 7

a I love making cakes.
b My brothers love playing basketball. All the players on their team are great!
c My friend likes going on the internet and looking at Facebook.
d We like going out and dancing.
e She's trying on a dress. She likes the design. She wants to buy it!
f Maya loves listening to music. Kanye West is her favourite singer.
g I like watching the news, but I don't like watching programmes about art.

GRAMMAR like + -ing

3 Complete the sentences with the correct form of the words in brackets. Use the present simple.

1 *Do you like living* (you / like / live) in the city?
2 Peter .... (not like) the Old Town. .... (you / like) it?
3 We .... (love / go) to the gym.
4 Stella .... (like) modern art.
5 My brothers .... (not like / clean) their flat.
6 My wife .... (love) new clothes.

4 Look at the underlined word in the sentences. Tick (✓) if the word is correct, or write the -ing form.

1 Tom likes play football. *playing*
2 My sisters don't like sport. ....
3 My husband loves his office. ....
4 Do you like stay in hotels? ....
5 I like visit different countries. ....
6 Mia doesn't like the local food. ....
7 We love go to the cinema. ....

5 Write sentences with these words. Use the correct verb form.

1 I / not like / drive / in the city.
   I don't like driving in the city.
2 they / like / watch / programmes about modern art.
   ....
3 we / love / do / exercise / at the gym.
   ....
4 you / like / swim / in the sea?
   ....
5 Peter / not like / look at / Facebook.
   ....
6 Danielle / love / cook / Chinese food.
   ....

DEVELOPING CONVERSATIONS
Me too and *I prefer*

6 **Read the conversations. Which people like the same things (S)? Which people like different things (D)? Write S or D.**

1 A: Do you like Jay-Z?
   B: He's OK, but I prefer his wife, Beyoncé. She's my favourite singer.   *D*
2 A: I love doing exercise.
   B: Me too. Which gym do you normally go to?   ....
3 A: Do you like reading magazines?
   B: I prefer reading stories.   ....
4 A: I love watching football.
   B: Me too. What's your favourite team?   ....
5 A: I go on the internet a lot.
   B: Me too. I like watching music videos.   ....

7 **Complete the conversations so they are true for you. Write *Me too* or *I prefer* … and your own ideas.**

1 A: I like going to the cinema.
   B: ....
2 A: I love cooking.
   B: ....
3 A: I love looking at Facebook.
   B: ....
4 A: Do you like the band called the Foo Fighters?
   B: ....

LISTENING

8 🔊 7.1 **Listen to three conversations. What did the men do yesterday? Match the photos (a–c) with the conversations (1–3).**

Conversation 1   picture [ ]
Conversation 2   picture [ ]
Conversation 3   picture [ ]

Learner tip

Listen to English every day. Listen to the news on the radio, listen to music and watch TV and films.

9 🔊 7.1 **Listen again. Are the sentences true or false? Circle T or F.**

Conversation 1
1 The woman doesn't like reading.   T   (F)
2 The man prefers reading books.   T   F
3 The man didn't read *The Year of the Flood*.   T   F
Conversation 2
4 The man didn't go out yesterday.   T   F
5 The man usually goes running on Sunday afternoons.   T   F
6 The woman prefers the band from South Korea.   T   F
Conversation 3
7 The man watched TV at a friend's house.   T   F
8 The woman knows the programme called *Father Brown*.   T   F
9 The man prefers English series.   T   F

VOCABULARY Country adjectives

Language note

We can say the country we are from:
I'm from China.
Or we can use an adjective to say our nationality:
I'm Chinese.

1 Complete the nationality words in the table with the endings in the box.

-an	-ese	-ian	-ish	-n

Country	Nationality
Brazil	¹ Brazil**ian**
China	² Chin___
Egypt	³ Egypt___
Italy	⁴ Ital___
Japan	⁵ Japan___
Mexico	⁶ Mexic___
Poland	⁷ Pol___
Russia	⁸ Russia___
Spain	⁹ Span___
The UK	¹⁰ Brit___
The US	¹¹ America___

2 Complete the sentences with nationality words from Exercise 1.
1 I love the US. I love everything *American*!
2 Leo Tolstoy was from Russia. He's my favourite .... writer.
3 The band called White is from the UK. It's my favourite .... band.
4 There are lots of dances in Spain. The most famous is flamenco, but I love all .... dancing.
5 I went to Japan on my last holiday. I really like .... food.
6 Manaus is a place in Brazil. It's an important .... city.
7 Chihuahuas are from Mexico. They're very small .... dogs.
8 Hossam Habib is a singer from Egypt. He writes and sings .... songs.

PRONUNCIATION /ən/, /iən/ and /ʃən/

3 Read these words and think about the sound of the letters in bold. What are the three different sounds?

American	Brazil**ian**	Egyp**tian**
Ital**ian**	Mexic**an**	Rus**sian**

4 ◐ 7.2 Listen and write the words in the table.

/ən/	/iən/	/ʃən/
American		

5 ◐ 7.2 Listen again and repeat.

GRAMMAR
Present continuous (*I'm* and *are you ...?*)

6 Complete the conversations with the words in the box. Use the present continuous.

do	~~listen to~~	look at	make
you / do	you / play	you / read	

1 A: What are you doing?
  B: I*'m listening to* my favourite song.
2 A: What are you doing?
  B: I .... sandwiches for lunch.
3 A: .... any good games at the moment?
  B: Yes, a lot!
4 A: What are you doing?
  B: I .... some exercise.
5 A: What are you doing?
  B: I .... a website about writers on the internet.
6 A: .... a good story at the moment?
  B: Yes, it's a great story.
7 A: What .... ?
  B: I'm dancing!

Language note

You use the **present continuous** for activities you are doing **now** or **at the moment**.
I'm making an Italian dish at the moment.
You use the **present simple** for activities you do **every day**, **always**, **usually**, etc.
I usually make Italian food at the weekend.

7 Tick (✓) the correct sentence (a or b).

1 a   What are you doing every day?   [   ]
  b   What are you doing now?   [✓]
2 a   Are you watching anything good on TV now?   [   ]
  b   Are you often watching anything good on TV?   [   ]
3 a   I'm a writer. I'm usually writing stories
     for children.   [   ]
  b   I'm a writer. I'm writing a story for children
     at the moment.   [   ]
4 a   What are you cooking at the moment?   [   ]
  b   What are you usually cooking?   [   ]
5 a   I am doing exercise at the gym now.   [   ]
  b   I am sometimes doing exercise at the gym.   [   ]

READING

8 Read the article from a website. Match the names of the series/films (1–3) to the nationalities (a–c).

1 *House*   a British
2 *Call the Midwife*   b Japanese
3 *Shall We Dance*   c American

9 Answer the questions. Write *C* for *Call the Midwife*, *H* for *House* or *S* for *Shall We Dance*. Which series/film is about:

1 someone who works in an office?   <u> S </u>
2 people from a long time ago?   ....
3 a man who has a job in a hospital?   ....
4 someone who helps mums and their families?   ....
5 someone who people don't like?   ....
6 someone who learns to do something?   ....
7 life in London?   ....
8 someone who changes during the story?   ....

10 Are the sentences true or false? Circle T or F.

1 Netflix only has films about the UK.   T   F
2 You can watch Netflix on any TV.   T   F
3 Antonia prefers American films.   T   F
4 Midwives are a type of nurse.   T   F
5 Dr House helps people in his job.   T   F
6 *Shall We Dance* is sad at the end.   T   F

11 Now read the article again and check.

I love Netflix™!
by Antonia Branca

I don't really like watching programmes on TV, but I love watching things on Netflix! You need the internet to watch Netflix, but it doesn't usually cost very much. Netflix has new films and series every month – they're from a lot of different countries.

I usually watch two or three series at the same time. I'm watching a series called *Call the Midwife* at the moment. It's about nurses in the UK in the 1950s and 1960s. The nurses (called *midwives*) help mothers and babies in an area of London, in England.

I'm also watching a series called *House*. It's about a doctor. His name is Gregory House and he works in a big hospital in New Jersey in the US. No-one really likes Dr House. Often he's not very nice, but he's always there for people that aren't well and need his help.

I don't only watch series on Netflix. Last night, I watched an interesting film called *Shall We Dance?* It's about a man and his problems. The man's name is Shohei Sugiyama and he lives in Tokyo, in Japan. He doesn't like his life or his job in an office. He's very sad, but then he goes to dancing lessons and he meets new friends. His life changes and he's happy.

Are you watching anything good at the moment? No? Try Netflix!

GRAMMAR *this/these, one/ones*

1 Tick (✓) all the sentences you can use to talk about each photo.

1
a This one looks good.   [✓]
b These are my size.   [ ]
c This is my size.   [✓]
d These ones look good. [ ]

2
a These are cool!   [ ]
b I love these ones!   [ ]
c I love this one!   [ ]
d This is cool!   [ ]

3
a Are these half price?   [ ]
b I prefer the blue one.   [ ]
c Is this half price?   [ ]
d I prefer the blue ones. [ ]

4
a Do you have these in a 12? [ ]
b Do you have this in a 12? [ ]
c These ones are medium.   [ ]
d This one is medium.   [ ]

2 Complete the sentences with *this*, *these*, *one* or *ones*.
1 I'm not sure about the colour of *this* one.
2 This is a beautiful jacket, but I prefer the red ....
3 .... jumper is very nice.
4 Try this .... It's a medium.
5 .... trousers are a bit long.
6 Look at these .... They have a great design.
7 These shoes are expensive. I prefer the cheap ....
8 These .... look comfortable, but try them.

VOCABULARY *Buying clothes*

3 Complete the words in the sentences with the vowels (*a, e, i, o, u*).
1 These gr *e* *e* n socks have twenty-five p__rc__nt off! That's a good reason for buying them!
2 I like this bl__ __ jumper, but my friend prefers the br__wn shirt.
3 This c__ __t feels c__mf__rt__ble and I really like the colour.
4 This dr__ss is very expensive and I'm not sure about the d__s__gn.
5 Do you have these trousers in an __xtr__ l__rg__?

4 Circle the correct words.
1 This *price / jacket* feels a bit small. I think I need a 38.
2 I love this *half / white* top, but it isn't my size.
3 The *yellow / long* trainers are great!
4 Look! This hat is *half / small* price.
5 I have a job in a bank. We can't wear *jeans / socks* and *shirts / T-shirts* to work.
6 My new shoes look *good / small*. I love them!
7 This skirt is very *black / long*. It's the wrong size.

DEVELOPING CONVERSATIONS Opinions

5 Complete the words in the conversations.
1 A: W*hat* do you think of this skirt?
    B: It's OK, but it's a b__ __ long.
2 A: Look at this shirt. What do you t __ __ __ __ ?
    B: Sorry. I don't r __ __ __ __ __ __ like it.
3 A: What do you think of these jeans?
    B: They're OK, but I'm not sure a __ __ __ __ the design.
4 A: What do you think of the jumper?
    B: I really l __ __ __ __ it! It looks great!
5 A: What do you think of the trainers?
    B: They're nice, but I'm not s __ __ __ about the price.

6 ♪ 7.3 Listen and check your answers.

DEVELOPING WRITING Writing a blog

7 Complete the sentences with the correct form of the verbs in brackets.
1 Jonathan *goes* (go) to the gym every day.
2 I .... (love) doing exercise.
3 Maria .... (make) lunch at the moment. She's hungry.
4 They .... (study) English at university when they were younger. Now, they are teachers.
5 We .... (not like) going to the cinema, but we like watching films at home.

Language note

Use **present simple**
to talk about things you normally do, and what you like and don't like.
Use **present continuous**
to talk about things you are doing at the moment.
Use **past simple**
to talk about things you did in the past.

8 **Read the text quickly. Is it:**
a an email?   b a story?   c a blog?

> Hi, everyone! Hans here!
>
> Today, I'm writing about one of my favourite people ... ME!
>
> I'm a university student and I'm studying [1] **English** because I want to be a teacher. In one of my classes, I'm learning about writers and their books. I love reading and I read a lot. At the moment, I'm reading a book called [2] .... It's by the American writer, Jonathan Franzen. It's about a family with a lot of problems.
>
> At the weekend, I love going out. I like playing [3] .... at home, but I prefer going to concerts and listening to [4] .... with my friends. Last weekend I saw a really good band in the city.
>
> I don't like the [5] .... on TV very much, but there are some good films and [6] .... on Netflix. I like watching them in the evening.
>
> And you? What are doing at the moment? I want to know about you!

9 **Complete the text in Exercise 8 with these words.**

bands	~~English~~	games	programmes
series	*The Corrections*		

10 **You want to write a blog about you. Complete the notes.**
I'm a .... I'm studying .... / working in ....
I love .... At the moment, I'm ....
It's ....
At the weekend, I love .... with
....
Last weekend, I ....
I like .... , but I prefer ....
I don't like .... but I love ....

11 **Write a blog about you. Use your notes from Exercise 10. Use the model text in Exercise 8.**

Vocabulary Builder Quiz 7

Download the Vocabulary Builder for Unit 7 and try the quiz below. Write your answers in your notebook. Then check them and record your score.

1 **Write the nationalities.**
1 Italy   ....
2 Mexico   ....
3 China   ....
4 Egypt   ....
5 the US   ....

2 **Circle the correct words.**
1 Thank you for my birthday *present / series*. I love it!
2 He's a really good *writer / singer*. They sell his books in many countries.
3 I love *cooking / running* in the park with my friends.
4 My favourite colours are *brown / modern* and blue.
5 It's Friday. Do you want to *try on / go out* tonight?

3 **Complete the words in the sentences.**
1 LeBron James is my favourite basket............................ player.
2 I use Faceb............................ a lot. It helps me at work.
3 This webs............................ has good information about the government.
4 I'm wearing a T-s............................ today because it's a hot day.
5 My flat is on the top f............................ of that building.

4 **Circle the word that is different in each group.**

1 dress	cake	jacket
2 politics	magazine	story
3 team	sport	prison
4 business	concert	band
5 exercise	toy	gym

5 **Complete the sentences with the words in the box.**

cheap	comfortable	famous	sad	vegetarian

1 This is a .... dish – it has no meat in it.
2 Look! That's the .... actor, Ryan Gosling!
3 Don't be ...., Monica. It's going to be a great day!
4 These jeans are .... – only €12!
5 This coat's not .... It's too small.

Score _____ /25

Wait a couple of weeks and try the quiz again.
Compare your scores.

HERE AND THERE

VOCABULARY Collocations

1 Look at the example and find six more verbs in the wordsearch. Use them to complete the collocations.

G	L	U	G	N	J	F	N	U	D
R	N	F	E	S	L	Z	L	H	P
M	E	E	T	Y	S	T	P	I	D
X	Z	S	C	H	A	X	T	L	F
S	A	W	O	R	K	M	A	C	A
T	C	D	Q	T	E	L	K	N	Z
U	T	R	A	V	E	L	E	M	U
D	E	Y	N	Z	B	T	W	Z	Q
Y	J	R	S	H	V	Z	P	A	Z
K	I	E	J	Y	M	A	K	E	E

1 *get* a coffee
2 .... an exam
3 .... Law at university
4 .... hard
5 .... a long way
6 .... a list
7 .... a client

2 Read the pairs of sentences. Complete both sentences with the same verb. Use the verbs from Exercise 1.

1 a I don't like my job. I want to **get** a new one.
  b We can go to that restaurant to **get** something to eat.
2 a Some of my friends .... in a factory.
  b I .... at home and I really like it.
3 a They want to .... to Japan next year.
  b My parents .... a lot for work.
4 a You need to .... hard at school.
  b I can't go to the cinema. I need to .... for an exam.
5 a I'm hungry. I'm going to .... a sandwich.
  b They're doctors. They .... a lot of money every week.
6 a I'm going to the gym at five o'clock. I'll .... you there.
  b We can .... in a café in the main square.
7 a We need to .... a friend to the airport.
  b It's cold today. I'll .... a coat with me.

GRAMMAR Present continuous: all forms

3 Circle the correct words.
1 What **'s** / 're your brother studying at university?
2 Is Maria *come* / *coming* to the party?
3 Oh, no. It **'s** / 're raining!
4 My daughter *'re not* / *'s not* going to the office today.
5 My tablet's not *work* / *working*.
6 *Are* / **Is** they having problems at the moment?
7 My husband's *playing* / *play* football today.
8 We *'re* / *'s* having a coffee now.
9 *Are* / **Is** the dog sleeping outside?
10 She's *staying* / *stay* in a hotel tonight.

4 Rewrite the sentences. Write positive sentences (✓), negative sentences (✗) or questions (?).
1 Is your sister going to the gym now?
  ✓ *Your sister is going to the gym now.*
2 I'm not taking a coat with me today.
  ✓ ....
3 It's raining in London at the moment.
  ✗ ....
4 Your son's not studying for an exam now.
  ? ....
5 Are they having a party today?
  ✗ ....
6 We're waiting for Jan to arrive.
  ? ....
7 Her phone's not working.
  ✓ ....
8 Are you travelling to New York today?
  ✗ ....

5 Use the verbs in the box to complete the sentences. Use the present continuous.

make	meet	not feel	not rain
they / come	you / travel		

1 *Are you travelling* to Wales by bus or train?
2 I .... a client at four o'clock.
3 It's my birthday. My daughter ....
   me a big cake!
4 James and Miranda are really nice –
   .... to your party?
5 My dad .... well. He didn't go to
   work today.
6 We can go to the park now. It ....

DEVELOPING CONVERSATIONS
Sending messages

6 Complete the sentences with the words in the box.

hello	I'm	say	sorry	thank

1 A: Her daughter's having problems at school.
   B: Really? Say *I'm* sorry.
2 A: I'm going to call Mum later.
   B: Oh, OK. .... hi.
3 A: These cakes are from my sister.
   B: Really? Say .... you.
4 A: I'm going to see Daniel later.
   B: Oh, really? Say ....
5 A: His wife's not feeling well.
   B: Oh, OK. Say I'm ....

LISTENING

7 🔊 **8.1** Listen to three conversations. Match the conversations (1–3) with the information (a–c).
   a Someone wants to know how a person is.   [   ]
   b Some people are late for something.   [   ]
   c Someone talks on the phone.   [   ]

8 🔊 **8.1** Listen again. Circle the correct words.
   Conversation 1
   1 Fran has a *son* / *daughter*.
   2 David is Fran's *brother* / *client*.
   3 David *can* / *can't* come to the meeting tomorrow.
   4 David wants to meet on Friday *morning* / *afternoon*.
   Conversation 2
   5 John is *a Spanish* / *an English* teacher.
   6 John *is making* / *isn't making* a lot of money.
   7 John's sister is visiting him next *week* / *Wednesday*.
   Conversation 3
   8 *Adam* / *Sofia* is on the train.
   9 The weather is *good* / *bad*.
   10 The cinema is *near* / *far from* the station.

9 🔊 **8.1** Complete the sentences with one word. Listen again and check.
   1 David is going on a *trip*.
   2 Fran is going to .... a client.
   3 John is .... in a school.
   4 John .... the US.
   5 The film starts at seven ....
   6 Sofia is .... from the station.
   7 Sofia didn't take a ....

PRONUNCIATION /ɪŋ/

10 Read these words and think about the sound of the letters in bold. What is the sound?

gett**ing**	mak**ing**	meet**ing**	study**ing**
tak**ing**	travell**ing**	work**ing**	

11 🔊 **8.2** Listen and repeat.

12 Can you think of five more words that have this sound?
....
....

VOCABULARY In the house

1 Complete the sentences with the words in the box.

bed	carpet	chair	cupboard	~~fridge~~
shelf	shower	sink	sofa	table

1 There's cold water in the *fridge*.

2 We usually have dinner at this ....

3 I'm hot, I'm going to have a ....

4 He's going to sit on the .... and watch TV.

5 The room is small. It only has a ....

6 I just cleaned the kitchen ....

7 There's nothing in this ....

8 I put some books on this ....

9 Here's a .... – do you want to sit?

10 Do you like this .... ? I want it for my room.

2 Complete the words for rooms.

1 The towels are in the cupboard next to the shower, in the b............................. .
2 There's a bed and a red carpet in my b............................. .
3 There's a fridge and a sink in the k............................. .
4 There's a sofa and some big chairs in the l............................. ....

GRAMMAR Personal pronouns

3 Read the text and complete the table.

Hi Anna! I want to tell you about my new flat – it's great! I share it with two friends, Sebastian and Lydia. I like living with them. Sebastian has a small room. We don't often see him because he studies a lot. Lydia's room is nice and big and she has a TV. I sometimes watch TV with her. I have a table and a chair in my room. My mum gave them to me.

Personal pronouns	
Subject pronouns	**Object pronouns**
1	me
2	you
3	it
he	4 ....
5	her
they	6 ....

4 The words in bold are incorrect. Write the correct words.

1 This is my brother, Stephan. He goes to your university. Do you know **her**? ...*him*...
2 I'm going to the cinema this evening and my friend, Jim, is coming with **them**. ....
3 These are my parents. They're great. I'm going to have lunch with **him** now. ....
4 You have a lot of presents! Who gave them to **me**? ....
5 This is my flat. **He**'s not very big, but I love it. ....
6 I'm having coffee with Stella later. **It**'s my friend. Do you want to meet her? ....

DEVELOPING CONVERSATIONS
Maybe

5 🔊 8.3 Listen and complete the conversations with the words in the box.

a ten-minute walk	at two o'clock	home
~~on the train~~	Saturday night	

1 A: Where did you last see your tablet?
  B: I can't remember. Maybe *on the train*.
2 A: When did you last see your friend, Suli?
  B: I'm not sure. Maybe ....
3 A: How far is your university from here?
  B: I don't know – not far. Maybe ....
4 A: Where's Kim today?
  B: I'm not sure. Maybe she's at ....
5 A: What time were you in the café?
  B: I'm not sure. Maybe ....

READING

6 Read the four texts. Are they about:

a different places to live?   [ ]
b different countries?   [ ]
c different families?   [ ]

> **Learner tip**
>
> When you read you often find words that you don't know – don't worry! Look at the word. Is it a noun (e.g. *chair, sofa*)? Is it a verb (e.g. *get, make*)? Or is it an adjective (e.g. *big, beautiful*)? Read the words next to the word you don't know. They will help you understand it.

7 Are the sentences true (T), false (F) or doesn't the text say (DS)? Circle T, F or DS.

1	Jackie isn't living in the city now.	⊤	F	DS
2	She lives on a quiet street.	T	F	DS
3	She has some shelves in her bedroom.	T	F	DS
4	Sahil is sharing a flat at the moment.	T	F	DS
5	He is living in the city.	T	F	DS
6	The living room is his favourite room.	T	F	DS
7	Brittany lives with her family.	T	F	DS
8	She has a red chair in her room.	T	F	DS
9	She has a table in her room.	T	F	DS
10	Vassilis is living with his mother.	T	F	DS
11	He lives in a new house.	T	F	DS
12	He can see something nice from his house.	T	F	DS

8 Now read the texts again and check.

Home is where the ♥ is! Why do you love your home? Tell us about it!

I live in a small house in a village called Ditchling. I love it because it's on a quiet street. I used to live in a big city and there was always a lot of noise! I didn't like that. My house is small but I have everything I need. There are four rooms: a kitchen, a living room, a bathroom and my bedroom. My favourite room is the kitchen. It's orange and I love the colour. It has a table and chairs and nice pictures on the walls.

Jackie

I don't have my own place, so I'm staying in my friend Rajeet's flat at the moment. The flat's in the city centre. I like the living room because it has two big windows, so it gets a lot of sun. It's a really nice room. The flat also has a small kitchen, two bedrooms and a bathroom. It's great for two people because we can sit and talk together when we want, but we can go to our own rooms when we want to study or read.

Sahil

I'm sharing a really nice flat with three friends at the moment. The flat's new and in a good area of Boston, in the US. I have my own bedroom. I have a bed and a chair in my room, but I can't have a table in there because my room's very small. But that's OK because we have a big living room and we all like to sit in there and watch TV or listen to music.

Brittany

I live with my wife and children in a house in Athens, Greece. The house is nice, but very old. My mother's mum – my grandmother – gave it to me. There are six rooms in the house. We have a living room with a beautiful red sofa, a kitchen with a big fridge and lots of cupboards, a bathroom and three bedrooms. From the kitchen window, we have a great view of Athens!

Vassilis

08

VOCABULARY Verbs and people

1 Complete the verbs in the sentences. Then answer the questions.

1 My friend c*leans* houses.
  What is he? *a cleaner*
2 Naomi's job is to t............................. English.
  What is she? ....
3 My wife d............................. a bus.
  What is she? ....
4 My husband m............................. a lot of workers in a big company.
  What is he? ....
5 I p............................. football to make money.
  What am I? ....
6 My sister w............................. books.
  What is she? ....
7 Jacob d............................. clothes for five different shops.
  What is he? ....

2 Label the photos with the jobs in Exercise 1.

1 *writer*   2 ....

3 ....   4 ....

5 ....   6 ....

3 Complete these sentences about jobs so they are true for you. Change words if you need to.

1 I am a .... I ....
2 My mum is a .... She ....
3 My brother is a .... He ....
4 My best friend is a .... He ....

PRONUNCIATION /g/, /dʒ/ and silent *g*

4 🔊 **8.4** Listen to these words. Do the letters in bold sound the same or different? Or do they have no sound (silent letters)? Write the words in the table.

designer	**g**ood	mana**g**er

/g/	/dʒ/	silent *g*
	Argentina	

5 🔊 **8.5** Listen to these words and write them in the table in Exercise 3.

Argentina	change	daughter	get	glasses
green	gym	high	sign	

6 🔊 **8.5** Listen again and repeat the words.

DEVELOPING WRITING
Describing a photo

Language note

A lot of words in English have silent letters (letters we don't hear or say). When you learn the words, learn the correct spelling. When you write in English, remember to spell the words correctly.
The letters in bold are silent.

desi**g**ner   **w**rong   frie**n**d   listen

7 Circle the silent letters.

1 I'm sorry. I don't know the answer.
2 My wife has a business – a lot of people work there.
3 Can you guess what's in that cupboard?
4 What does it say on that sign?
5 Are you writing an email to your mum?
6 I can climb that high mountain!

8 🔊 **8.6** Listen and check.

9 Look at the photo on page 51 and read the text quickly. What do you think the woman's job is? Choose the best answer.

a a manager
b a teacher
c a writer

In the photo, I can see a [1] *woman* – she's working. There's a pen and a computer on a table in front of her. But I don't think she's in an office because I can see a TV and a [2] .... in the room. I think the woman is in a [3] .... or flat. I think she's in her [4] .... and she's homeworking. I don't know what her job is. Maybe she's a [5] .... and she's writing a book or a story at the [6] ....

10 Complete the description with these words.

house	living room	moment
sofa	woman	writer

11 Now look at this photo. Complete the notes to describe the photo. Use the description in Exercise 9.

In the photo, I can see .... She is .... There are ....
I don't think .... because
....
I think the .... is in ....
I say that because .... I can see
....
I don't know .... Maybe she's a
.... and she is .... at the moment.

12 Describe the photo. Use your notes from Exercise 11. Use the model text in Exercise 9.

Vocabulary Builder Quiz 8

Download the Vocabulary Builder for Unit 8 and try the quiz below. Write your answers in your notebook. Then check them and record your score.

1 Circle the correct words.
1 Do you *remember / get* what her name is?
2 I need to *say / call* my office. I can't work today.
3 My wife *grows / designs* dresses for her friends.
4 I want to *move / sell* this table. I want £20 for it.
5 What time do you *leave / come* work every day?

2 Circle the word that is different in each group.

1 shelf	card	cupboard
2 bag	sink	shower
3 sofa	chair	runner
4 bedroom	kitchen	parent
5 key	designer	project manager

3 Complete the words in the sentences.
1 You can't drive when you're fifteen. That's the l........................... .
2 They make cars in a big f........................... in my town.
3 I went to the supermarket, but I didn't buy everything on my l........................... .
4 I'm hungry. Is there any food in the f...........................?
5 Pizza is my favourite Italian d........................... .

4 Complete the sentences with the words in the box.

company	glasses	message	pictures	way

1 My son loves to draw .... Look. This one is a cat!
2 I need to wear ...., but only when I drive.
3 I travelled a long .... today – I'm very tired.
4 I can send you a .... when I get to London.
5 Jake manages a big .... in Poland.

5 Match the beginnings (1–5) with the endings (a–e).
1 That's a nice carpet. I have a similar
2 People are looking everywhere for my lost
3 I think your book is in the living
4 My sister is a professional
5 Does your friend have his own

a singer. She's very good.
b one in my office.
c room on the table.
d website?
e dog.

Score ___/25

Wait a couple of weeks and try the quiz again. Compare your scores.

VOCABULARY Parts of the body

1 Look at the pictures and complete the crossword.

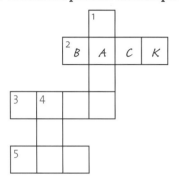

Across →

Down ↓

2 Complete the words with the vowels (a, e, i, o, u).
1 You cut your h__nd.
2 He br__k__ his l__g.
3 I h__d a very b__d c__ld.
4 He h__d a h__ __d__ch__ .
5 She f__lt s__ck.
6 You h__t your h__ __d.
7 I h__rt my b__ck.
8 She h__d something __n her __y__ .
9 You br__ke__ your __rm.

> **Learner tip**
>
> When you write a new word in your vocabulary notebook, you can draw a small picture next to it to help you remember what it means.
>
> eye

3 Which health problems did you have in the past? Tick (✓) the sentences. Change words if you need to.
1 I cut my ~~hand~~.   leg   [✓]
2 I had something in my eye.   ....   [ ]
3 I hit my head.   ....   [ ]
4 I felt really sick.   ....   [ ]
5 I really hurt my back.   ....   [ ]
6 I broke my arm.   ....   [ ]
7 I had a cold.   ....   [ ]
8 I had a bad headache.   ....   [ ]

GRAMMAR Time phrases for the past

4 Circle the correct words.
1 a few *days* / *day* ago
2 *this* / *last* morning
3 *a few* / *on* Monday
4 twenty *minute* / *minutes* ago
5 *on* / *last* night
6 *on* / *ago* Friday
7 three *weeks* / *week* ago
8 *last* / *on* month
9 *last* / *this* afternoon
10 five *year* / *years* ago

5 Complete the conversations with *ago, few, last* or *this.*
1 A: I went shopping for new clothes.
   B: Oh? When was that?
   A: Two days *ago*.
2 A: I lost my keys.
   B: Oh, no! When was that?
   A: .... morning.
3 A: I got married.
   B: Oh! When was that?
   A: .... year.
4 A: I got a new job.
   B: Great! When was that?
   A: A .... months ago.
5 A: I made our booking.
   B: OK. When was that?
   A: .... Monday. A week ago.
   B: That's good. Thank you.

6 Look at the sentences that you ticked in Exercise 3. Say when they happened. Use the time phrases from Exercises 4 and 5 and your own ideas.
....
....
....
....
....
....

DEVELOPING CONVERSATIONS
Are you feeling better?

7 Complete the conversations with the words in the box.

bit	much	~~OK~~	really	thanks

1 A: Is your leg *OK* now, Petros?
  B: Not really.
2 A: Hi, Mo. Are feeling better?
  B: Yes. .... better, thanks.
3 A: Are you feeling better, Sophia?
  B: A .... better.
4 A: Is your back OK now, Martina?
  B: Much better, ...
5 A: Are you feeling better, Takis?
  B: Not ....

LISTENING

8 🍂 9.1 Listen to four conversations. Who had a problem with their health? Tick (✓) the name(s).

1	2	3	4
John	Lee	Steven	Dylan
Pam	Chan	Ivan	Lin
			Joe

9 What can you remember about the people? Write answers to the questions.

Conversation 1
1 Who went to the Philippines?
  John and Pam.
2 Who felt sick?
  ....
3 When did he/she feel sick?
  ....

Conversation 2
4 Who went to the gym?
  ....
5 What problem did Chan have?
  ....
6 When didn't Chan go out?
  ....

Conversation 3
7 Who does Steven meet for the first time?
  ....
8 Where does Ivan think Steven works?
  ....
9 When did Steven hurt his back?
  ....

Conversation 4
10 What is Lin's husband's name?
  ....
11 Where did he have an accident?
  ....
12 When did he have an accident?
  ....

10 🍂 9.1 Listen again and check.

PRONUNCIATION long and short *a* and *o*

11 🍂 9.2 Look at the letters of the alphabet and listen to how they sound.
A B C D E F G H I J K L M N O P
Q R S T U V W X Y Z

12 🍂 9.3 Now listen to the vowels (a, e, i, o, u).

Language note

In English, the vowels can have long or short sounds.

When the vowel sound is like the letter of the alphabet, then it's a long vowel, e.g.

n**a**me, h**o**me

When the vowel sound isn't like the letter of the alphabet, then it's a short vowel, e.g.

h**a**ppy, c**o**nference, **o**ffice

13 Read these words and think about the sound of the letters in bold. What are the four different sounds?

convers**a**tion	s**a**fe	b**a**ck	h**a**nd
c**o**ld	br**o**ke	d**o**ctor	h**o**spital

14 🍂 9.4 Listen and write the words.

long *a*	short *a*	long *o*	short *o*
conversation	....	....	
....	....	....	

15 🍂 9.4 Listen again and repeat.

VOCABULARY Country and society

1 Circle the word that is different in each group.
1 **education:** teacher school (sun)
2 **health system:** university doctor hospital
3 **safe:** crime operation police
4 **weather:** countryside rain snow
5 **environment:** water air war

2 Complete the sentences with words from Exercise 1.
1 I love sun, and rain is OK, but I really don't like *snow*! It's cold!
2 There is a lot of .... in this area of the city, but the police can't do anything about it.
3 Everyone needs a good .... It's very important to have great schools and great .... to work in them.
4 We need to help the .... Clean air and .... are really important.
5 I cut my hand this morning. I needed to go to .... and see a(n) ....
6 My dad broke his back and needed a(n) .... I'm happy we have a really good health .... in our country.

3 Write sentences about your country. Use the ideas in Exercise 2.

....
....
....
....
....

GRAMMAR Quantity

4 Write the words in the box in the correct place.

| a lot | almost no | lots | no | quite a lot | some |

90% 1 *a lot* / 2 ....
70% 3 ....
40% 4 ....
10% 5 ....
0% 6 ....

5 Look at the numbers in brackets. Complete the conversations with words from Exercise 4.
1 A: Education here is very bad.
  B: I know. There are *no* universities in this city. (0%)
2 A: Is the weather nice in your country?
  B: Yes, we have .... snow, but not very much. (40%)
3 A: Is this a bad area?
  B: Yes, there's .... of crime here. (70%)
4 A: The people in this village have a big problem.
  B: Yes, there's .... clean water near here. (10%)
5 A: Did you visit a doctor today?
  B: Yes, I had .... of headaches last week. (90%)

6 Choose the correct answers.
1 There .... lots of good people on my street.
  a have (b) are c is
2 There .... a lot of crime in my city.
  a is b are c have
3 There .... almost no women doctors at this hospital.
  a is b have c are
4 We .... quite a lot of clean water in Canada.
  a are b have c is
5 There .... no hospitals in this town.
  a have b is c are
6 There .... a lot of rain in Britain.
  a is b have c are
7 We .... some beautiful mountains in my country.
  a is b are c have

READING

Language note

A *fact sheet* is a piece of paper which gives information about something.

7 Read the three fact sheets on page 55 quickly. What things do they talk about?

	Denmark	Lebanon	Japan
education			
environment	✓		
food			
health system			
sport			
weather			

Denmark is a happy country – second in the world! There are lots of reasons for that.

- Denmark has lots of fresh air and clean water. It also has beautiful islands, beaches, lakes and forests.
- The Danish think that family and friends are very important. They love staying in and going out together. One of the things they love to do is watch football. Football is Denmark's favourite game. At the moment, there are 300,000 players and 1,614 teams in Denmark.

Fun fact: The Danish have a special word for feeling comfortable and happy because you're together with people you really like – it's *hygge*.

Japan is a small country with about 127 million people living there. That's a lot of people, but it's a great country to live in.

- Japan has some of the best hospitals in the world, and they don't cost anything! The doctors are very good and Japanese people usually live for a very long time.
- The Japanese think that going to school and studying hard is very important. Japanese students usually do really well in exams. They know that going to university helps them get jobs and have better lives.

Fun fact: The Japanese name for Japan is *Nihon* or *Nippon* which means 'from the sun'.

Lebanon is a very old, beautiful country. People started to build villages there about 7,000 years ago.

- Lebanon has lots of sun in the summer, with some rain. In December, there's some snow in the mountains.

- The Lebanese love food – making it and eating it! They love to sit and share food with others. The Lebanese eat quite a lot of chicken and lamb with fresh vegetables.

Fun fact: A favourite dish in Lebanon is called *baba ghanoush* – people make it with a vegetable called an aubergine.

8 What do you remember about the fact sheets? Answer the questions.
1 In Denmark, which sport do people really like? *Football.*
2 Can you drink the water in Denmark? Why? / Why not?
3 Can you go swimming in Denmark? Why? / Why not?
4 When did people start to build villages in Lebanon?
5 What kinds of meat do Lebanese people often eat?
6 Where does it snow in Lebanon?
7 Does Japan have a good health system? Why? / Why not?
8 What is important for people in Japan?
9 Why do people in Japan think going to university is important?

9 Now read the texts again and check.

VOCABULARY Meeting and moving

1 Match the beginnings of the sentences (1–8) with the endings (a–h).

1 We met when we were on   *b*
2 I moved here for   ....
3 My wife and I worked together in   ....
4 We both work in tourism and we met at   ....
5 We were in   ....
6 I came to the UK to   ....
7 We're in Tokyo on   ....
8 Tom and I did our Master's   ....

a a conference.
b holiday in China.
c at the same university.
d my last job – she was my boss!
e business. We have an important client here.
f the army together.
g study. I'm going to be a doctor.
h work. This is where my company is now.

2 Circle the correct words.

1 A: Why are you here in London, Magda?
   B: (To study) / For work. I'm doing a Master's here.
2 A: *Why are you here? / How do you know each other?*
   B: Oh, my husband was a friend of Youssef.
3 A: Why are you here, Roshan?
   B: For *love / business*! My wife is from Spain – and the food here is better!
4 A: Why are you here?
   B: I'm here on *work / business*. I'm meeting a client.
5 A: How do you know each other?
   B: We were at *army / university* together. We did the same course.
6 A: Why are you here in Toronto, Eva?
   B: For *work / love* My new office is here.
7 A: How do you know each other?
   B: We *studied / met* together at the University of Oxford.

3 Think of four people you know. Say how you know them.

Example: *Zoe*
       We worked together in my last job.

1 Name: ....
....
2 Name: ....
....
3 Name: ....
....
4 Name: ....
....

DEVELOPING CONVERSATIONS
Have you been ...?

4 Number the parts of each conversation.

1 a Yes, three years ago.   [   ]
   b What did you think of it?   [   ]
   c Have you been to Romania?   [*1*]
   d It was beautiful!   [   ]
2 a Where did you go?   [   ]
   b To lots of interesting places.   [   ]
   c Have you been to Brazil before?   [   ]
   d Yes, last year.   [   ]
3 a Have you been here before?   [   ]
   b Three days.   [   ]
   c Yes, last month.   [   ]
   d How long were you here?   [   ]
4 a No, never. And you?   [   ]
   b Why did you go?   [   ]
   c Yes, a few months ago.   [   ]
   d Have you been to Uruguay?   [   ]
   e On business.   [   ]

DEVELOPING WRITING
Writing an email

Language note

When we write emails, we need to use the correct beginnings and endings for the person we are writing to.

For family and friends:
Beginnings: Hello, ... / Hi, ...
Endings: Bye, ... / Love, ... / Write soon, ...
For someone we don't know well:
Beginnings: Dear ...,
Endings: Best wishes, ... / Kind regards, ...

5 Complete the table with the words in the box.

| Best wishes, | Bye, | Dear, | Hello, | Hi, |
| Kind regards, | Love, | Write soon, | | |

Beginnings	Endings
	Best wishes,

6 Read the email. Choose the correct ending to complete the sentence.

Last week, Joanna:

a had a bad cold. [　]

b cut her hand. [　]

c hurt her back. [　]

Sent　Chat　Attach　Font

Hi Aliyah,

How are you? I'm really well. I love living abroad – Wales is great. It's cold here now, but I love the rain and snow.
I really like my university – the teachers are great. The university's in a good area and I'm very safe when I walk there from my flat every morning.
I'm sharing the flat with my new friend, Joanna – she's from the US and we do the same course at university.
Last week, she had a very bad cold and she had to go to hospital. But it was OK because the hospitals in Wales are really good and it doesn't cost anything to see a doctor. She's much better now.
I'm taking exams at the moment. I'm studying quite a lot, but now I need a break – I want some fresh air.
I'm sending a photo. Write soon,
Zara

7 Imagine you are living abroad and you want to write an email to a friend. Choose a place you know or a place you want to visit. Look at the model email. Complete the notes with similar information.

I .... living abroad.

.... is ....

The weather here is ....

I'm living .... with

....

I really like .... because

....

Last week, I ....

I'm .... at the moment.

8 Write your email. Use your notes from Exercise 7 and the model email in Exercise 6. Remember to use the correct beginning and ending.

Vocabulary Builder Quiz 9

Download the Vocabulary Builder for Unit 9 and try the quiz below. Write your answers in your notebook. Then check them and record your score.

1 Circle the correct words.

1 Can you open the window? I need some fresh *air / environment*.

2 My brother's in the *conference / army*, so he goes to places where there are wars.

3 I'm going to Japan on *course / business* next week.

4 Ow! I have something in my *eye / back*!

5 We have *quite / almost* a lot of crime in my city.

2 Complete the words in the sentences.

1 Dad works long hours. He needs more free t.............................

2 Did you watch the World C.............................? My favourite team won!

3 I don't like living in the city. I want to live in the countrys.............................

4 We have a really good health s............................. in my country. We don't pay to see a doctor.

5 I have a heada............................. Can I go home?

3 Complete the sentences with the words in the box.

hand	police	street	summer	weather

1 I was cooking and I cut my ....

2 There's someone in the house. Call the ....

3 How's the .... there today? Is it hot?

4 I live on this .... – in that yellow house.

5 I love the sun, so I love ....

4 Match the beginnings (1–5) with the endings (a–e).

1 I'm not feeling　　a my teacher why I was late.

2 I told　　b in a hotel in London?

3 I broke　　c my leg and now I can't go on holiday.

4 Did you stay　　d your head when you hit it?

5 Did you hurt　　e well. I need to see a doctor.

5 Complete the sentences with words formed from the words in brackets.

1 My parents want me to have a good .... (educate)

2 It's .... here. There isn't much crime. (safe)

3 My mum's in hospital. She needs an .... (operate)

4 Sorry you're sick. I hope you're .... soon! (good)

5 There's a .... lake in my town. (beauty)

Score ___/25

Wait a couple of weeks and try the quiz again.
Compare your scores.

10 NEWS

VOCABULARY Summer and winter

1 Are the phrases about summer (S) or winter (W)?

1 it's 36°C   S
2 have a fire   ....
3 turn on the air-con   ....
4 it's cold and rainy   ....
5 turn on the heating   ....
6 it's hot and dry   ....
7 it's −38°C   ....
8 it's going to snow   ....
9 it's sunny   ....
10 it's warm   ....

2 Complete the sentences with the words in the box.

air-conditioning	change	degrees	fire
heating	~~minus~~	stay	summer
sunny	wet	windy	winter

1 It's very cold – it's *minus* 40!
2 I don't like cold and snow, so I don't like ....
3 Is it going to .... hot like this all week?
4 I don't have .... in my flat because it's not normally very hot here.
5 It's 25 .... here today. What's the weather like where you are?
6 It's a ...., rainy day, so I don't want to go to the park.
7 It's a very .... day. Be careful on your bike.
8 The weather's going to .... tomorrow – it's going to snow!
9 I love the sun, so I love the ....
10 I'm cold. Can you turn on the ...., please?
11 On cold days, we often have a .... in the living room.
12 It's very .... today. Don't sit on the beach for long.

3 Put the words in the correct order to make sentences.

1 ? / snowing / it / now / is
   Is it snowing now?
2 today / horrible / cold / it's / and
   ....
3 a / it / here / rains / lot
   ....
4 wet / was / winter / very / here / it / last
   ....
5 ? / yesterday / London / did / rain / it / in
   ....

VOCABULARY EXTRA *Like*

4 Choose the correct answers.

1 The weather here .... the weather in my country.
   (a) is like   b likes
2 Is it going to .... this all week?
   a look like   b stay like
3 Everyone says I .... my sister. We are both quite small.
   a stay like   b look like
4 What's the weather going to .... like tomorrow?
   a be   b stay
5 That cat .... a bit like my cat. They both have green eyes.
   a looks   b stays

GRAMMAR Future: *am/are/is going*

5 Match the sentences (1–6) with the responses (a–f).

1 It's very hot today!
2 I'm going to Venice at the weekend.
3 Tony's going to have a barbecue this evening.
4 It's going to snow tomorrow.
5 Are Mum and Dad going shopping today?
6 He's a very bad driver.

a I know, he bought all the food yesterday.
b Really? It's not very cold.
c Yes, they're going after work.
d I know. He's going to have an accident.
e Yes, and it's going to stay like this for three days.
f Great! How much was the ticket?

6 Complete the sentences with 'm, 're or 's.

1 It**'s** going to be sunny tomorrow.
2 I......... going to my friend's house at the weekend.
3 We......... going skiing in the mountains next week.
4 He......... going camping on Sunday.
5 Your team is great! You......... going to win the game!
6 They......... going to be here later.

7 Complete the sentences with the verbs in brackets. Use the correct form of *be going to*.

1 It's raining. You**'re going to get** (get) wet.
2 I .... (do) some exercise at the gym this evening.
3 Lina .... (have) dinner with me later – she made a cake!
4 The weather .... (stay) like this for the next two days.
5 They .... (take) the train to the city tomorrow.
6 Tobias .... (play) football this evening. He's a great player.

DEVELOPING CONVERSATIONS

I think so / I don't think so

> **Language note**
> -
> In informal English, people often pronounce *going to* as *gonna* ('gənə). You can use *gonna* when you're talking to family and friends, but you can't use it when you're talking to people you don't know very well. You should never use it in writing.

8 Complete the conversations with the words in the box.

do	don't	going	is	so	think

1 A: *Is* the weather going to stay like this?
  B: I think so.
2 A: Is it .... to be really hot in August?
  B: I think so.
3 A: Does your teacher have children?
  B: I .... think so.
4 A: .... your friends have any plans for the weekend?
  B: I think so.
5 A: Are you going on holiday in the summer?
  B: I don't think ....
6 A: Is it going to snow in November?
  B: I don't .... so.

9 Answer the questions in Exercise 8 for you. Use *I think so* or *I don't think so* and add another sentence.
1 *I think so. They say it's going to be hot all next week.*
2 ....
3 ....
4 ....
5 ....
6 ....

LISTENING

10 🔊 10.1 Listen to Miguel talking to Carol. Match the people (1–5) with the plans (a–e).
1 Miguel   *d*
2 Carol   [ ]
3 Loretta   [ ]
4 James   [ ]
5 Lucas   [ ]

a go skiing
b make dinner
c go shopping
d go swimming
e have a barbecue

11 🔊 10.1 Listen again. Are the statements true (T) or false (F)?
1 Carol loves wet weather.   T (F)
2 Carol can drive.   T   F
3 Miguel talked to Loretta last night.   T   F
4 It's very hot in Australia.   T   F
5 James is Miguel's brother.   T   F
6 England and Spain are having the same weather at the moment.   T   F
7 Lucas is working in the mountains.   T   F
8 Lucas likes the snow.   T   F
9 Miguel loves skiing.   T   F
10 Miguel doesn't have a pool.   T   F

VOCABULARY Entertainment

1 Circle the correct words to label the pictures.

1 play / **fair**   2 band / match

3 circus / film   4 comedy show / festival

5 film / classical concert

2 Complete the sentences with the words in the box.

band	concerts	exhibition	play	shows

1 My favourite singer is Rihanna and my favourite **band** is Imagine Dragons.
2 We're going to the theatre to see a(n) .... next week.
3 My parents love going to classical .... , but I don't like that kind of music.
4 My brother really likes comedy ....
5 I'm going to the modern art .... tomorrow. Do you want to come?

3 Are the sentences true (T) or false (F)?

1 We can go to the cinema to watch a film.   (T)   F
2 A circus is a kind of game like football.   T   F
3 People play matches at the theatre.   T   F
4 Bands play music.   T   F
5 Children can't go to fairs.   T   F
6 One kind of exhibition is a photo exhibition.   T   F

4 Do you like these kinds of entertainment? Number them 1 to 10 (1 = love, 10 = hate).

bands	[ ]	fairs	[ ]
circuses	[ ]	festivals	[ ]
classical concerts	[ ]	films	[ ]
comedy shows	[ ]	matches	[ ]
exhibitions	[ ]	plays	[ ]

DEVELOPING CONVERSATIONS
Deciding what to do

5 Circle the correct words.

A: Do you have plans for the weekend, Thomas?
B: No, nothing special. And you?
A: No, I don't have any plans. Do you want to go somewhere and listen to some music?
B: ¹ **Yeah** / No, great.
A: ² When / How about a club? Glorious Sons are playing at Club 22 tonight.
B: I don't really like clubs. I ³ prefer / 'd prefer a concert in the park.

A: Are you doing anything on Saturday, Meghan?
B: No, I don't think so. Do you want to do something together?
A: ⁴ Oh / OK. How ⁵ about / but a classical concert?
B: I don't ⁶ very / really like classical concerts. I ⁷ 'm / 'd prefer a comedy show. There's one at the café on Maple Street on Saturday night.
A: OK. I'm going shopping at five. I ⁸ 'll meet / meet you after that.

6 🔊 **10.2 Listen and check.**

PRONUNCIATION
Long and short vowel sounds: *e* and *u*

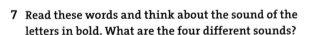

Language note

Remember that in English, the vowels (*a, e, i, o, u*) can have long sounds and short sounds.

7 Read these words and think about the sound of the letters in bold. What are the four different sounds?

m**ee**t   h**e**   h**e**lp   sp**e**nd   m**u**sic   J**u**ne   s**u**n   cl**u**b

8 🔊 **10.3 Listen and write the words.**

long *e*	short *e*	long *u*	short *u*
....	....	....	*club*
....	....	....	....

9 🔊 **10.3 Listen again and repeat.**

READING

10 Read the interview in the article quickly. What do Janet and Ian talk about? Write ✓ and ✗.

a Where the festival is.   [   ]
b When the festival is.   [   ]
c What you can see and do at the festival.   [   ]
d How much the festival costs.   [   ]

11 What do you remember about the interview? Answer the questions.

1 When is the festival? *August.*
2 Where is the festival? ....
3 When did the festival start? ....
4 How many shows were there the first year? ....
5 How many shows were there last year? ....
6 What kind of show does Ian like best? ....

7 How long does the festival last? ....
8 How's the weather in August in Scotland?
....
9 Where's Ian going to see a music show?
....
10 When's Ian's show? ....

12 Now read the interview again and check.

13 Answer the questions so they are true for you.

1 Do you think the Fringe is fun? Why? / Why not?
....
2 What things can you do at the Fringe?
....
3 Are they things that you like to do? Why? / Why not?
....
4 Do you have a festival like the Fringe in your country?
....

Summer Fun for Everyone!

by Janet McClean

Yes, it's August in Scotland again, and to many people that means one thing – it's time for the Edinburgh Festival Fringe! I talked to Ian Cameron, a local comedian, about this great festival.

Janet: Hi, Ian! Thanks for talking to me today. First, I wanted to ask you about how the festival started – can you tell us about that?

Ian: Yes, I can, Janet. I'm from Scotland – Edinburgh – and I do shows at the Fringe, so I know a lot about it! The Fringe started in 1947, and in its first year there were only eight theatre companies there.

Janet: Really? The Fringe is a lot bigger now!

Ian: Yes, it is! Last year, there were 3,398 shows!

Janet: Tell us, Ian, what kinds of things can you do there?

Ian: Well, lots of things. You can go to plays and exhibitions. You can see circus shows, music shows, dance shows, children's shows – and my favourite – comedy shows.

Janet: Where can you do these things?

Ian: All over Edinburgh!

Janet: Great! How long does the Fringe last, Ian?

Ian: It starts on 3rd August and it lasts for three weeks.

Janet: And what's the weather usually like in August in Scotland?

Ian: The weather's sometimes warm and dry – usually it rains.

Janet: Well, thank you, Ian. What are you going to see this week?

Ian: Well, I'm going to see my favourite band play on the Royal Mile.

Janet: When do you do your show?

Ian: Next Friday – in Appleton Towers at Edinburgh University!

Janet: Great! I'll meet you there!

> **Glossary**
>
> **comedian:** a person who does comedy shows

VOCABULARY
National and international news

1 Choose the correct response (a–e) to the sentences (1–5).
1 Scott paper is going to close its factory in the US.
2 Real Madrid lost 1–0 to Man United.
3 There was an election in my city last week.
4 Princess Agatha is going to get married.
5 There was a really big fire in a cinema near here.

a How did it start?
b How many people work there?
c Great! When is that going to be?
d Who scored?
e Who won?

2 Choose the correct option.
1 Her grandfather *died* / *scored* two years ago. He had *an election* / *a heart attack*.
2 A: Monaca LaTrek *closed* / *had* her *baby* / *factory*.
  B: Is it a boy or a girl?
3 There was a big *accident* / *heart attack* in town yesterday. Four people died.
4 They're going to *build* / *lose* a new airport near here.
5 The government is going to *win* / *spend* more money on hospitals.
6 There was a *princess* / *fire* near here last year. The mountain is all black now.
7 When is your brother getting *married* / *scored* to Susan?
8 A: Did you watch football on TV last night?
  B: Yes, my team won and my favourite player *scored* / *built*!
9 The *accident* / *factory* in my town makes cars.

GRAMMAR Past forms review

3 Find ten past forms in the wordsearch.

E	Q	N	W	I	P	V	W	Y	N
T	S	E	A	M	M	H	H	A	L
O	F	W	Q	G	V	A	R	Z	D
O	I	W	N	E	L	P	W	C	E
K	N	G	O	T	C	P	A	O	C
K	I	A	C	W	L	E	S	P	I
R	S	A	T	O	O	N	Z	E	D
K	H	D	R	N	S	E	L	N	E
L	E	W	C	R	T	D	K	E	D
S	D	S	T	O	P	P	E	D	D

4 Complete the table with the words from the wordsearch.

Present	Past	Regular or irregular?
be	*was*	*Ir*
decide		
finish		
get		
happen		
lose		
open		
stop		
take		
win		

5 Which of the verbs in the table are regular (R)? Which are irregular (Ir)? Write *R* or *Ir* in column 3 of the table.

6 Complete the pairs of sentences with the verbs in bold. Use the past form.
1 **talk   cut**
  a My favourite football player *cut* his leg during the match yesterday.
  b The police *talked* to all the people on my street last night.
2 **help   come**
  a The American president .... to my city two days ago.
  b The government .... ten villages last month.
3 **cost   try**
  a The new hospital in Texas .... over $800 million to build.
  b They .... to open a new factory in my area three years ago.
4 **spend   use**
  a They .... £55 million on the new airport last year.
  b It was a big forest fire – they .... a lot of water to stop it.
5 **play   meet**
  a The two presidents .... on Tuesday to talk about the environment.
  b Lionel Messi .... in the World Cup in Russia.

DEVELOPING WRITING
Writing a postcard

> **Language note**
>
> When you write, you can make your writing more interesting by using different adjectives.

7 Circle the correct adjective.
1 My hotel room is small, but it's very *clean* / *boring*.
2 We can sit by the fire and stay *angry* / *warm* and dry.
3 Neymar is a really *fun* / *famous* football player – he scores a lot.
4 That's a beautiful *old* / *sad* theatre; I like going there.
5 I love going to museums in London – they're very *interesting* / *boring*.

8 Read the postcard quickly and underline thirteen adjectives. How does Noel begin and end his postcard?

> Hello Beatrice!
> Here I am in beautiful Jamaica. I'm staying in a small hotel in Negril and I'm having a great time. It's hot and sunny – 29 degrees – here today, and it's going to stay like this for the next three or four days. There's a beautiful beach near the hotel – it's busy, but the sea is really warm. Yesterday, I met some interesting people from Croatia. We went to see a local band – it was fun! I'm going to have dinner with them tonight and we're going to Montego Bay tomorrow. We're going to go to the main square and have a coffee – a cold one!
> Back next week; I'll meet you then.
> Bye for now,
> Noel

9 You are going to write a postcard to a friend. Tick (✓) the things you can talk about. Then write notes for each one.

a country [ ]
....

b where you are staying (hotel, hostel, etc.) [ ]
....

c all the things you took with you on your trip [ ]
....

d the weather [ ]
....

e the things you did [ ]
....

f how much money you spent on food [ ]
....

g things you plan to do [ ]
....

10 Write your postcard. Use your notes from Exercise 9. Use the model text in Exercise 8.

Vocabulary Builder Quiz 10

Download the Vocabulary Builder for Unit 10 and try the quiz below. Write your answers in your notebook. Then check them and record your score.

1 Circle the correct words.
1 How much did it *last* / *cost* to build the new stadium?
2 The jazz band is playing in the *second* / *main* square.
3 Do you want to go and see a *play* / *fair* at the theatre?
4 What's the weather going to be *about* / *like* tomorrow?
5 We really liked the exhibition. It was *fun* / *dry*!

2 Complete the words in the sentences.
1 On hot, sunny days, I often use the air-.............................
2 My parents really like classical m............................., but I don't.
3 Do you want to go to a comedy s............................. tonight?
4 I need to go to the wash r............................. . Back in a minute.
5 Oh, no! Tom had a heart a.............................!

3 Complete the sentences with the phrases in the box.

close the club	die in an accident	get wet
stay warm	win the match	

1 I don't want to go out. I'm going to .... in front of the fire.
2 It's 1–1. If we score again we're going to ....
3 She didn't .... – she had cancer.
4 My cat doesn't go outside when it rains. She doesn't want to ....
5 They .... at 11pm on Monday nights.

4 Match the beginnings (1–5) with the endings (a–e).
1 Can you turn on
2 I don't like circuses. I prefer
3 How much does the government spend
4 I want to do something for our anniversary – maybe
5 Can you turn off

a the heating? It's hot in here.
b on health services per year?
c the TV, please? I want to watch a film.
d festivals.
e have a barbecue or go to a restaurant.

5 Complete the sentences with words formed from the words in brackets.
1 We have a new president. The .... was last week. (elect)
2 I don't want to go to the beach. It's a very .... day. (wind)
3 We're going .... in the mountains next weekend. (ski)
4 They are having a .... about the environment at the moment. (discuss)

Score ___ /25

**Wait a couple of weeks and try the quiz again.
Compare your scores.**

LIFE AND HISTORY

VOCABULARY Months

1 Write the months in the box in the correct order.

April	August	December	February
~~January~~	July	June	March
May	November	October	September

1 *January*
2 ....
3 ....
4 ....
5 ....
6 ....
7 ....
8 ....
9 ....
10 ....
11 ....
12 ....

2 Look at the calendar for July. Complete the phrases for the times on the calendar. Use the words in the box.

beginning	during	end	first	~~in~~
last	middle	second or third		

1 ☐ + ◼ + ◼
   a *in* July
   b .... July

2 ☐
   a at the .... of July
   b in the .... week of July

3 ◼
   a in the .... of July
   b in the .... week of July

4 ◼
   a at the .... of July
   b in the .... week of July

July						
Mon	Tues	Wed	Thurs	Fri	Sat	Sun
1	2	3	4	5	6	7
8	9	10	11	12	13	14
15	16	17	18	19	20	21
22	23	24	25	26	27	28
29	30	31				

3 Match (1–8) with (a–h).

1 the first	*c*	a 3rd
2 the second	[ ]	b 11th
3 the third	[ ]	c 1st
4 the fifth	[ ]	d 23rd
5 the eleventh	[ ]	e 17th
6 the seventeenth	[ ]	f 28th
7 the twenty-third	[ ]	g 2nd
8 the twenty-eighth	[ ]	h 5th

4 Circle the correct words.

I can't wait for **1st** August! I have a lot to do ¹(during)/ *middle* the month of August. At the ²*end / beginning* of August, on the **4th**, it's my parents' anniversary and we're having a big party to celebrate. In the ³ *last / middle* of the month, on the **16th**, it's my brother's birthday and we're taking him to a nice restaurant for dinner. Near the ⁴ *middle / end* of the month, on the **24th**, it's a public holiday and I'm going to the beach with friends. In the ⁵ *last / second* week of August, on the **26th**, I'm going on holiday to Portugal!

5 Look at the dates in bold in Exercise 4. Write the words for the dates.

1 *the first*
2 ....
3 ....
4 ....
5 ....

Language note

We can also write dates as numbers, but be careful!
They are different in the UK and the US.
In British English, we write the day, then the month:
11th April 2018 = 11/04/18
In American English, we write the month, then the day:
April 11th 2018 = 04/11/18

GRAMMAR Questions review

6 Put the words in order to make questions.

1 ? / cinema / does / want / Dan / come / the/ to / to
   Does Dan want to come to the cinema?

2 ? / Bill / party / why / at / wasn't / yesterday /the
   ....

3 ? / party / to / you / can / come / my / parents'
   ....

4 ? / going / be / how / your / old / is / sister / to
   ....

5 ? / to / are / dinner / going / with / who / you
   ....

6 ? / you / celebrate / doing / to / anything / are
   ....

7 ? / what / for / his / did / get / your / birthday / husband / you
   ....

8 ? / summer / did / go / last / anywhere / you
   ....

7 The words in bold in the questions are wrong. Write the correct words.

1 **What** was the holiday terrible? What happened? *Why*
2 **Where** old is your daughter going to be? ....
3 **Why** is going to be at the meeting this afternoon? ....
4 **Did** you help me with my work, please? ....
5 **How** did you go on your birthday last year? ....
6 **Is** your friend want to come to the festival with us today? ....
7 **Do** Stella going to do anything to celebrate her new flat tomorrow? ....
8 **Who** did you get your wife for your anniversary? ....
9 **Were** they go anywhere on Saturday? ....

8 Match the questions (a–e) with the sentences (1–5). Then write the full question in each conversation.

1 A: My sister's birthday is on Tuesday.
   B: *c How old is she going to be*?
2 A: I'm going to a conference in Berlin.
   B: ....?
3 A: Is there a problem, Demitris?
   B: Yes. ....?
4 A: My sister got married last week.
   B: ....?
5 A: My holiday was horrible.
   B: ....?

a you / help me with my homework
b why / it / horrible
c how old / she / going to be
d she and her husband / do anything to celebrate
e who / you / going with

Developing Conversations
Invitations

9 Complete the words in the four conversations.

1 A: We're having a barbecue on Saturday. *Can* you and your wife come?
   B: Maybe. I need to c_ _ _ _ _ . Can I call you later?
   A: OK
2 A: I've finished my exams, so I'm going to have a party. D _ _ you want to come?
   B: I'd l_ _ _ _ to. What d_ _ _ ?
   A: Saturday.
   B: Oh, no. Sorry, I c_ _ _ ' _ . I'm going away for work.
   A: OK.

3 A: I need a weekend away, so I'm g_ _ _ _ camping. Do you want to c_ _ _ _ ?
   B: Sure. What d_ _ _ _ _ ?
   A: The 5th and 6th.
   B: Great!
4 A: There's a conference in Madrid next week. Can you come?
   B: M _ _ _ _ _ . What day?
   A: Next Friday.
   B: OK, I think so, but I need to check my d_ _ _ _ _ .

10 ◔ 11.1 Listen and check your answers.

Listening

11 ◔ 11.2 Listen to Tonya and Ali talking. Tick (✓) the things they talk about.

a public holiday	[ ]		an anniversary	[ ]
a birthday party	[ ]		a conference	[ ]
a meeting	[ ]		a barbecue	[ ]

12 What can you remember about the conversation? Complete the notes.

Ali's birthday party
Name of restaurant: [1] *Luigi's*
Kind of food: [2] ....
Where: [3] ....
Date: [4] ....

Tonya and Larry's anniversary
How many years married: [5] ....
Date: [6] ....
Kind of party: [7] ....
Time: [8] ....
Address: [9] ....

Conference
Where: [10] ....
Go on: [11] ....
Come back on: [12] ....
Tonya's boss goes on: [13] ....

13 ◔ 11.2 Listen again and check.

VOCABULARY Life events

1 Circle the phrase that is not a correct collocation with the verb in bold.

1 **go:**   into the army   to prison   of a heart attack
2 **become:** university   a doctor   famous
3 **move:**   to the countryside   a new life   to the UK
4 **lose:**   your job   a degree   money
5 **finish:** an online shop   school   working
6 **live:**   in a nice area   on the streets   interested in art
7 **do:**   a Master's   well at school   divorced
8 **die:**   in an accident   married   in her sleep

2 Choose the word in the box that completes all three sentences (a–c).

| become | get | have | live | start | ~~was born~~ |

1 *was born*
   a Mum .... near here – in the hospital on Main Street.
   b I .... in a small village in Greece.
   c My father .... in the 1950s.
2 ....
   a When did your sister .... teaching at the university?
   b I don't want to work for someone else – I want to .... a business.
   c We went to America to .... a new life.
3 ....
   a Why does your brother .... a problem with the police?
   b My friend, Meghan, is going to .... a baby in June.
   c They .... an online shop. It sells concert tickets.
4 ....
   a Why did they .... divorced?
   b I want to .... a job in a big company in New York City.
   c When did your parents .... married?
5 ....
   a In this city a lot of people .... on the streets.
   b We .... in a nice area of Prague.
   c Joseph and Grant .... with their mother in a small flat.
6 ....
   a When did you .... interested in art?
   b She wants to go to university and .... a teacher.
   c When did Richard Gere .... famous?

3 Which of the things in Exercise 1 and 2 did you do? When? Write sentences.

....
....
....
....
....
....

Learner tip

You can use a dictionary to check the meaning of words, but when you write what a new word means in your vocabulary notebook, use your own words. Your own words are easier to remember.

GRAMMAR
Explaining when: time phrases

4 The words in bold in the sentences are wrong. Write the correct word: *after, in* or *when*.

1 **In** the terrible accident, I couldn't sleep.   *After*
2 Antonio was born **when** September 1981   ....
3 **When** the 1970s, this was a good area. It's not a good area now.   ....
4 Otto could read **after** he was four!   ....
5 Her three children were born **when** she moved to the US.   ....
6 **In** I was a child, I couldn't speak English.   ....

5 Complete the sentences with *after, in* or *when*.

1 *When* he was in the US, he lived in Washington.
2 He couldn't find a job .... he did his Master's.
3 His family moved house .... he was six. They moved house again the next year.
4 They got married .... they left university.
5 Dad went into the army .... the 1990s. He left the army in 1999.
6 We moved to the countryside .... 2014. That was a great year!
7 .... I was a child, I couldn't swim.
8 Debra had problems with the police .... 2000, but then she started a new life.

6 Number the sentences about a man's life in the order that they happened.

a After school he went to university and got a degree.   [ ]
b He retired in 2018 and now he lives in Spain.   [ ]
c He finished school in 1971.   [ ]
d After he got his Master's, he moved to the UK.   [ ]
e He sold the company and got a job in London.   [ ]
f His business had problems in 1985 and 1986 and he lost a lot of money.   [ ]
g Juan was born in Mexico City in 1953.   [*1*]
h When he was thirty he started a business.   [ ]

READING

7 Read about the people on the webpage quickly. Why are they famous? Circle the correct words.
1 Alexander Graham Bell   *inventor / writer*
2 Florence Nightingale   *nurse / doctor*

In this week's *Who's Who*, we look at two more famous people who have helped to change the way we live.

Alexander Graham Bell, the great inventor, was born in Scotland, on 3rd March, 1847. His mother and father taught him at home for a few years, but he also went to school and university. In 1870, Bell and his parents moved to Canada. The next year, Bell moved to the US where he started teaching people who couldn't hear, and in 1872 he started a school to help these people. During his years in the US, Bell worked on a new invention that was later called 'the telephone' and on 10th March, 1876 he used it to talk to someone for the first time. After a long, good life, Bell died in Nova Scotia, Canada on August 2nd, 1922.

Did you know? After Alexander Graham Bell died, telephone lines in the US and Canada were 'closed' for one minute – people couldn't use their phones. He was famous because of his invention.

Florence Nightingale was born in Florence, Italy on 12th May 1820. She moved to England with her family in 1821. When Nightingale was a child, there weren't a lot of schools for girls, so her father taught her at home. Nightingale always loved helping people and animals when they weren't well and, when she was 17, she knew that she wanted to become a nurse. She is famous because she understood that more people got better in clean hospitals. She changed people's ideas about health and being clean. Nightingale died on August 13th, 1910 – she was ninety.

Did you know? Florence Nightingale is called 'The Lady of the Lamp' because she didn't sleep very much and often visited people in hospital during the night with her lamp.

Glossary

inventor: a person who designs and builds new things
lady: a word for a woman that people used in the past
lamp: a kind of light

8 Circle the correct words.
1 Alexander Graham Bell was born on *the third / the thirty-first* of March.
2 He talked on the phone to someone for the first time in *1872 / 1876*.
3 He died in *Canada / Scotland*.
4 After he died, lots of people couldn't use their *cars / phones* for one minute.
5 Florence Nightingale was born on *the twentieth / the twelfth* of May.
6 She loved helping people and animals that were *sad / sick*.
7 She knew that hospitals need to be *clean / quiet*.
8 She didn't sleep a lot *because she was sick / so she visited sick people*.

9 Are the sentences true or false? Circle T or F. Correct the false sentences.
1 Alexander Graham Bell studied at home when he was a child.   Ⓣ   F
2 He moved to Scotland in 1870.   T   F
3 He was a teacher for people who couldn't hear.   T   F
4 He died in the winter.   T   F
5 Florence Nightingale moved to England with friends in 1821.   T   F
6 She went to school when she was a child.   T   F
7 She knew what job she wanted to do when she was 17.   T   F
8 She died in 1913.   T   F

10 Now read the texts again and check.

PRONUNCIATION /i/, /ɪ/ and /aɪ/

11 Read these words and think about the sound of the letters in bold. What are the three different sounds?

w**i**th	pr**i**son	bus**y**	outs**i**de	n**igh**t
d**ie**d	wh**y**	hungr**y**	histor**y**	

12 🔊 11.3 Listen and complete the table.

/i/	/ɪ/	/aɪ/
	with	

13 🔊 11.3 Listen again and repeat.

VOCABULARY History

1 Complete each sentence with one of the words in bold.

1 **high   big**
  a The Kuala Lumpur Tower is 421 metres *high*.
  b Russia and Canada are very *big* countries.

2 **killed   fought**
  a England .... with France 200 years ago, but they're friends now.
  b It's very sad, but a lot of people were .... in wars in the 20th century.

3 **repaired   damaged**
  a They .... my car yesterday, but today it's not working again!
  b Earthquakes .... homes and other buildings in Greece last summer.

4 **capital   main**
  a Do you want to go to the .... square and have a coffee?
  b I live in Spain, in the .... city, Madrid.

5 **castle   wall**
  a That's the .... where the King of Scotland lived.
  b You can't see the factory because there's a .... around it.

6 **king   queen**
  a Elizabeth I was .... of England for 44 years. She died in 1602.
  b Otto I was the .... of Greece, but he was born in Germany.

7 **century   year**
  a William Shakespeare, the famous writer, was born in the sixteenth ....
  b I was born in 1995 and my sister was born a .... later in 1996.

2 Complete the words in the sentences.

1 The CN Tower in Toronto, Canada is over 553 metres h*igh*.
2 Poland and Russia were at war in both the sixteenth and seventeenth c_ _ _ _ _ _ _ _ _.
3 My grandfather f_ _ _ _ _ _ _ in the Vietnam War. He says it was horrible.
4 In the old town, we walked along the city w_ _ _ _ _.
5 Henry VIII was the k_ _ _ _ of England for 38 years.
6 A man k_ _ _ _ _ _ the US president in 1865.
7 People built walls to p_ _ _ _ _ _ _ their towns.
8 The old theatre was d_ _ _ _ _ _ _ after the fire. It's going to cost a lot to r_ _ _ _ _ _ _ it.
9 A: What's the c_ _ _ _ _ _ _ city of England?
    B: London.

GRAMMAR
Explaining why: *because* and *so*

3 Complete the pairs of sentences with *because* or *so*. Add a comma (,) before *so*.

1 a I want to start a business *because* I like money!
   b I like money, *so* I want to start a business.
2 a They moved to the countryside .... they didn't like living in the capital city.
   b They didn't like living in the capital city .... they moved to the countryside.
3 a He killed someone .... he's in prison.
   b He's in prison .... he killed someone.
4 a The wall was damaged .... they are repairing it.
   b They're repairing the wall .... it was damaged.

4 Match the beginnings of the sentences (1–6) to the endings (a–f).

1 I'm going to university   [*d*]
2 My microwave isn't working   [   ]
3 My sister's in hospital   [   ]
4 The two countries are fighting   [   ]
5 They wanted to protect the old building   [   ]
6 We didn't like the government   [   ]

a because she's going to have a baby.
b so they built a high wall.
c so we had an election to change it.
d because I want to become a doctor.
e so I'm going to ask someone to repair it.
f because they are at war.

DEVELOPING WRITING
Writing an autobiography

5 The text on page 69 is a short autobiography. What is an autobiography for? Tick (✓) the correct answer.
a to write about a place   [   ]
b to write about your life events   [   ]
c to write about a time in history   [   ]

Wiesbaden

My Life (until now!)

by Gill Fulmore

I was born in Germany on 2nd September, 1985, but I'm not German. My father was in the American army and he worked in a place called Wiesbaden, in Germany. My parents lived there for two years and then they had a baby – it was me!

We moved back to the US in 1988, when I was three. When I was six I started school, and I finished when I was seventeen in 2002. I wanted to become a writer, so I went to university. After I got a Master's in 2007, I started working in a publishing house.

I met a man at work, and he became my husband – we got married on 1st July, 2014. We don't have any children now, but we plan to have lots!

6 Complete Gill's timeline with the words in the box.

1988   2007   finished school   got married   ~~was born~~

2nd September, 1985 ¹*was born*

²................... moved back to the US

2002 ³...................

⁴................... got a Master's

1st July, 2014 ⁵...................

7 Tick (✓) your life events.

was born	[ ]	started a business	[ ]
moved house	[ ]	went in the army	[ ]
started school	[ ]	travelled	[ ]
finished school	[ ]	got married	[ ]
went to university	[ ]	had a child/children	[ ]
got a degree	[ ]	other life event	
started a job	[ ]	....	[ ]

8 Write the life events that you ticked in Exercise 7 on the timeline. Add dates.

....

....

....

....

....

9 Write an autobiography. Use your timeline from Exercise 8 and the model text in Exercise 5. Remember to put your life events in the order that they happened.

Vocabulary Builder Quiz 11

Download the Vocabulary Builder for Unit 11 and try the quiz below. Write your answers in your notebook. Then check them and record your score.

1 Complete each word group with a word from the box.

anniversary   middle   prison   queen   second

1 beginning   end   ....
2 king   princess   ....
3 birthday   public holiday   ....
4 first   third   ....
5 school   castle   ....

2 Complete the sentences with the words in the box.

celebrated   fought   got   moved   was

1 My wife .... born on 2 September, 1989.
2 Steven .... his degree last year.
3 Tina and Scott got married. They .... by having a big party.
4 Frank .... house a month ago.
5 France and England .... each other many years ago.

3 Complete the words in the sentences.

1 My mum's mum, my grand..........................., is 73.
2 Maria, this is Sven. He's my boy...........................
3 I bought this charger from an on........................... shop.
4 We're going camping in the country........................... .
5 I'm tired. I don't want to go any........................... tonight!

4 Match the beginnings (1–5) with the endings (a–e).

1 I need to call someone because
2 Do they usually go out during
3 My brother started to change when
4 What kind of
5 How often do you go away

a on holiday?
b the printer's not working.
c he moved to the USA.
d the week?
e car do you drive?

5 Complete the sentences with words formed from the words in brackets.

1 He has a great life – he's a .... man! (luck)
2 She was late and her boss is .... (anger)
3 Jamaica became an .... country on 6 August, 1962. (dependent)
4 I'm .... in modern art. Are you? (interest)
5 I don't need to work this weekend. I want to go .... (where)

Score ___ /25

Wait a couple of weeks and try the quiz again. Compare your scores.

12 THANK YOU AND GOODBYE

VOCABULARY Offering solutions

1 Look at the pictures. Complete the sentences with the words in the box.

| broken | empty | heavy | lost | low | strong | working | wrong |

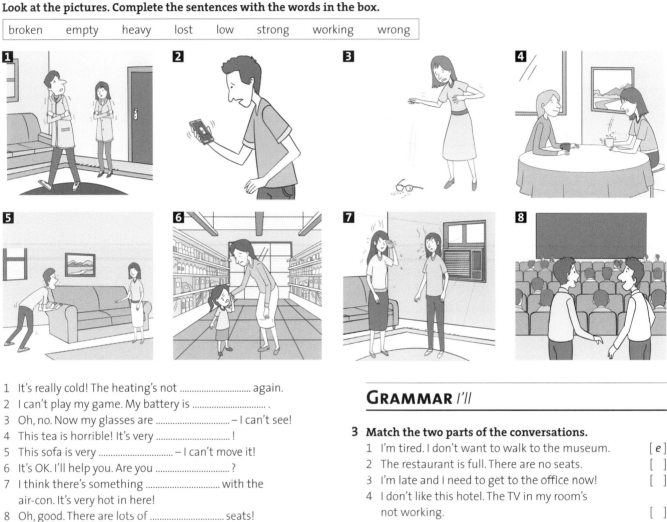

1 It's really cold! The heating's not .... again.
2 I can't play my game. My battery is ....
3 Oh, no. Now my glasses are .... – I can't see!
4 This tea is horrible! It's very .... !
5 This sofa is very .... – I can't move it!
6 It's OK. I'll help you. Are you .... ?
7 I think there's something .... with the air-con. It's very hot in here!
8 Oh, good. There are lots of .... seats!

2 Circle the correct words.

1 A: I want to move these chairs, but they're heavy.
   B: That's OK. I'll *carry* / *repair* them.
2 A: My phone's not working.
   B: Maybe it's your battery. Use my *seat* / *charger*.
3 A: I'm lost. Can you tell me where platform 12 is?
   B: I'm going there. I'll *lend* / *show* you.
4 A: I can't go to the circus. I have no money.
   B: I'll *carry* / *lend* you some.
5 A: My bike's broken.
   B: I'll *repair* / *show* it for you.
6 A: Oh, no. The restaurant is very busy.
   B: Don't worry. I'll go in and look for a *seat* / *charger*.

GRAMMAR *I'll*

3 Match the two parts of the conversations.

1 I'm tired. I don't want to walk to the museum.   [*e*]
2 The restaurant is full. There are no seats.   [   ]
3 I'm late and I need to get to the office now!   [   ]
4 I don't like this hotel. The TV in my room's not working.   [   ]
5 There are a lot of people on the bus. I don't think there are any empty seats.   [   ]
6 What time does the concert start this evening?   [   ]
7 This sandwich is horrible.   [   ]

a Don't worry. I'll take you to work if you want.
b I don't know. I'll check our tickets.
c Yes, you're right. I'll wait for the next one.
d Really? My burger's great.
e I'll go and get us a taxi, if you like.
f Oh, right, yes. It is very busy.
g My TV's fine. I'm watching the news now.

4 Look at sentences a–g in Exercise 3 again. Which three sentences do not offer a solution to the problem in 1–7? Write a better solution to the problem.

Sentence	Solution

5 Write an offer using *I'll* and one of the verbs in bold.

1 **check   send**
   A: My printer's broken.
   B: *I'll send* someone to look at it.

2 **repair   carry**
   A: My car's not working.
   B: .... it for you if you want. I know lots about cars.

3 **lend   show**
   A: I want to buy theatre tickets, but they're very expensive.
   B: .... you €30 if you like.

4 **take   go**
   A: I'm hungry.
   B: .... and order some cakes and drinks.

5 **wait   check**
   A: I don't know what time the football game is on TV.
   B: .... online if you want.

DEVELOPING CONVERSATIONS
Checking and thanking

6 Number the parts of each conversation 1–5.

1 a I'll turn on the air-conditioning.   [2]
  b Yeah. It's fine.   [4]
  c It's really hot in here.   [1]
  d Are you sure?   [3]
  e OK. That's great. Thanks.   [5]

2 a Yeah. It's fine. I like cooking.   [   ]
  b I didn't have dinner and I'm really hungry.   [   ]
  c Really? Are you sure?   [   ]
  d OK. Thanks.   [   ]
  e I'll make you something to eat, if you like.   [   ]

3 a Oh. That's great. Thanks!   [   ]
  b Are you sure?   [   ]
  c I'm a bit lost. Can you tell me how to get to the train station?   [   ]
  d Yeah, it's fine. I'm going that way.   [   ]
  e Of course. I'll show you where it is.   [   ]

LISTENING

7 🔊 **12.1** Listen to the conversations. Where are the people? Tick (✓) the correct answers.

Conversation 1
a at a barbecue
b in a café

Conversation 2
a in a car
b in a restaurant

8 What do you remember about the conversations? Tick (✓) the problems that the people have.

1 There are no seats.   [   ]
2 The cappuccino is very strong.   [   ]
3 The cakes aren't fresh.   [   ]
4 There are no chocolate cakes.   [   ]
5 The battery is low.   [   ]
6 The meeting is at one o'clock.   [   ]
7 The client is late.   [   ]
8 There's a lot of traffic.   [   ]

9 🔊 **12.1** What solutions did the speakers offer? Match the solutions with the problems you ticked in Exercise 8. Listen again and check.

a I'll stand.   [   ]
b I'll send someone to look at it.   [   ]
c I'll go and order you another one.   [   ]
d I'll carry it.   [   ]
e You can have mine.   [   ]
f I'll lend you my phone.   [   ]
g I'll take you.   [   ]
h I'll check the internet for you.   [   ]

PRONUNCIATION
long and short vowel sounds review

10 Look at the words in the box and think about the sound of the letters in bold. Write the words in the table.

b**a**ck	**cho**colate	com**pu**ter	c**o**ntact	g**e**t	h**o**me
h**o**pe	m**e**	pl**a**ce	s**a**fe	s**e**nd	st**u**ff
s**u**nny	t**a**xi	r**u**le	w**e**		

	long vowel sound	short vowel sound
a	*place, safe*	...................., ...
e	...................., ...	...................., ...
o	...................., ...	...................., ...
u	...................., ...	...................., ...

11 🔊 **12.2** Listen and check your answers.

12 🔊 **12.2** Listen again and repeat.

12

VOCABULARY EXTRA Gifts

1 Look at the photos and complete the crossword.

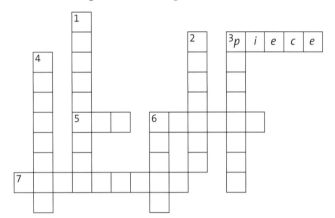

Across

3 a .... of art   5 a plastic ....

6 a box of ....   7 some ....

Down

1 a ....   2 some ....

3 a ....   4 a .... game

6 a ....

2 Complete the sentences with the words in the box.

book	chocolates	home-made	lovely
money	~~painting~~	sculpture	T-shirt

1 I love the *painting* on your wall. Is it a Picasso?
2 Joe thinks that .... cakes are a very nice gift.
3 Mum went to the Bahamas. She bought us all a .... with a picture of the sea printed on it.
4 She got a box of sweets *and* a box of .... for her birthday!
5 Maria gave us a .... about her country. It has beautiful photos.
6 We bought them a piece of art as a wedding gift – a .... of a cat.
7 When I finished university, Dad gave me some .... – £200!
8 Julia gave me a .... gift – two chairs for my garden!

3 What are good gifts for these people? Circle the best answer.

1 someone you work with
   a photos of your family   (b) a piece of art
2 your father
   a a home-made cake   b a plastic toy
3 a client from another country
   a a T-shirt with your photo printed on it
   b a big book about your city with lovely photos
4 a baby
   a a plastic toy   b a painting
5 your girlfriend/boyfriend
   a a photo of your mother   b a box of chocolates

Crossword across 3: `p i e c e`

GRAMMAR Explaining purpose: *for* or *to*

4 Circle the mistakes in four questions, and tick (✓) the questions which are correct.

1 Do you need anything for your headache? [✓]
2 Do you know anywhere to some good local food? [ ]
3 Do you ever buy flowers for say sorry? [ ]
4 Where's a good place to a wedding here? [ ]
5 Do you want to have lunch at this restaurant? [ ]
6 Where's the best place for go for a coffee? [ ]

5 Circle the correct words.

1 I bought a gift to /*for* my teacher. I wanted to thank her *to* / *for* her help in class.
2 We want *to* / *for* leave the music festival. There is nothing *for* / *to* the children *for* / *to* do here.
3 I went *for* / *to* the doctor's. I needed something *for* / *to* my cold.
4 I got my mum some flowers *for* / *to* her office.

DEVELOPING WRITING
Writing a letter about a problem

Language note
- -
When we talk or write about events, we use words like *first*, *then* and *in the end* to show the order of these events.

6 Circle the correct words.

I am writing about problems I had at your restaurant. [1] *First* / *In the end*, the food the waiter brought to our table wasn't what we ordered. [2] *Then* / *First*, when he brought the right food it was cold. [3] *In the end* / *First*, we left without waiting for dessert.

7 Read the letter about problems at a hotel. How does Gabriella begin and end her letter? Complete the letter with words from Exercise 6.

8 Imagine you had problems at a hotel. Tick (✓) the things you can include in a letter to the hotel. Then write notes.

1 where the hotel was [ ]
....
2 how you got to the hotel [ ]
....
3 the weather [ ]
....
4 the food at the hotel [ ]
....
5 your room at the hotel [ ]
....
6 a solution to your problem [ ]
....

220 Cumberland Road
Leeds
LS6 2EG

15 July

Dear Sir or Madam,

I am writing about a visit to your hotel in Corfu. I was there on holiday from 1st July to 7th July.

[1] F _ _ _ _, we arrived at the hotel. We were hot and we wanted to go to the beach, but it was a long way. We needed to get a taxi to get there, and it was busy and noisy.

[2] T _ _ _, we wanted to get something to eat – some special local dishes. Your hotel restaurant doesn't have any Greek food. It only has things like sandwiches, burgers and chips. In the [3] _ _ _, we went to a restaurant in the main square for local food.

I did not enjoy my visit and the holiday was expensive. I'll use a different travel company for my next holiday.

Yours faithfully,

Gabriella Hollis

9 Write a letter about your problems. Use your notes from Exercise 8. Use the model text in Exercise 7.
Remember to use words like *first*, *then* and *in the end* to put your ideas in order.

VOCABULARY
Leaving and saying goodbye

1 Circle the correct words.
1 I really *enjoyed* / *forgot* staying at your home.
2 Oh, no! I *ordered* / *forgot* my book!
3 Bye! *Need* / *Give* me a call!
4 I *hope* / *enjoy* we see each other again soon.
5 Oh! I *missed* / *forgot* my train.
6 I'll *give* / *order* you a taxi.
7 I *miss* / *need* to hurry. I don't want to be late.

2 Complete the sentences with the words in the box.

care	contact	everything	journey	kind
lovely	phone	quick		thanks

1 Oh, you bought me a bus ticket! That was *kind* of you.
2 You're back already. That was .... !
3 Here's some fruit and water for your ....
4 Well, goodbye! Stay in .... !
5 Do you have .... you need in your bag?
6 Hello, again! I forgot my ....
7 It was .... meeting you. Take .... !
8 .... for having me!

3 Are the sentences true or false? Circle T or F.
1 When you give someone a call, you send them a letter.   T   F
2 It's a problem when you miss a plane.   T   F
3 When you're late, you often need to hurry.   T   F
4 No-one likes kind people.   T   F
5 When you enjoy something, you like it.   T   F
6 When you need a taxi, you order one.   T   F
7 A journey is a kind of special local food.   T   F
8 Quick and fast mean the same thing.   T   F

GRAMMAR
Telling people to do things: Imperatives

4 Make sentences. Then answer with *I will* or *I won't*. In which conversations can you answer with *OK*?
1 home / you're / when / give / a / me / call
   Give me a call when you're home.
2 us / forget / call / don't / to
   ....
3 a / have / journey / good
   ....
4 too / don't / hard / work
   ....
5 ticket / your / forget / plane / don't
   ....
6 some / your / rest / holiday / get / on
   ....

5 Complete the sentences with the words in the box. Use the correct imperative form.

get	go	help	hurry	not ask	not be
not forget	not work	say			

1 *Help* your sister make dinner.
2 .... your tablet again. It's on the table.
3 .... late. We have a meeting.
4 .... hi to Martha and Bob!
5 .... and get a coffee now if you need to.
6 .... up. We're going to miss the film!
7 .... the boss now. He's with a client.
8 .... too hard. .... some rest.

Language note

We can use both *going to* and *will* to talk about what we are going to do in the future. But remember that we use *going to* for things we already planned and things we think are going to happen, and we use *will* for offering solutions and promising to do things.

READING

6 Read the first paragraph of the webpage quickly. Who can this website help? Tick (✓) the people.
1 businessmen and businesswomen who travel a lot   [ ]
2 people with families   [ ]
3 students studying in other countries   [ ]
4 people who work in other countries   [ ]
5 people on holiday   [ ]

7 Circle the correct words.
1 Brazilian people like *flowers* / *pens* for gifts.
2 Chinese people like *T-shirts* / *money* for gifts.
3 Indian people like *sweets* / *fruit* for gifts.
4 Japanese people like *money* / *pens* for gifts.

8 Answer the questions.
1 What's not a good gift for a Brazilian person?
   Anything they can cut their hand with.
2 Why isn't it a good gift?
   ....
3 When do Chinese people open their gifts?
   ....
4 What hand do you use to give an Indian person a gift?
   ....
5 How many times do you need to offer a gift in Japan?
   ....
6 Who likes fruit and jewellery for gifts?
   ....
7 Who likes T-shirts with the name of a country?
   ....
8 Who likes it when people give their sons and daughters toys?
   ....

9 Now read the webpage again and check.

12

International 'rules' for giving gifts

When we travel for work, studies or fun, we often buy gifts for the people we meet to thank them or say goodbye. Good idea! BUT you should know about the 'rules' for gifts in different countries.

Brazil
People in Brazil like to get things like flowers, fruit and jewellery for gifts.

Rule #1! Don't give a Brazilian anything they can cut their hand with. They think that a gift like that means you want to 'cut' being their friend!

China
People in China like it when people give them some money for a gift.

Rule #2! Don't worry when a Chinese person doesn't open their gift in front of you – Chinese people wait until the 'giver' leaves and then they open their gifts.

India
People in India like sweets, flowers and money for gifts. They also like it when people give their children toys.

Rule #3! Don't give an Indian person a gift with your left hand. Give it with your right hand or they often don't want it!

Japan
People in Japan like flowers, sweets and pens for gifts. They also like gifts that show where the 'giver' is from, so T-shirts with your country's name printed on it are great gifts.

Rule #4! Don't worry when a Japanese person doesn't take your gift the first time you offer it – you need to do it three times or they don't want to take it!

Vocabulary Builder Quiz 12

Download the Vocabulary Builder for Unit 12 and try the quiz below. Write your answers in your notebook. Then check them and record your score.

1 Complete the opposite words.
1. high ≠ l _ _
2. full ≠ e _ _ _ _
3. remember ≠ f _ _ _ _ _
4. horrible ≠ l _ _ _ _ _
5. slow ≠ q _ _ _ _

2 Circle the word you can't use with the word in bold.
1. **broken** — glasses — theatre — leg
2. **miss** — a seat — a train — a class
3. **offer** — a call — a solution — help
4. **lend** — money — books — a brother
5. **carry** — boxes — a sofa — space

3 Complete the sentences with the words in the box.

care	in	other	out	up

1. Can you help me stand ...., please?
2. Take ....! Have a safe trip!
3. I have a problem. The water in the shower is coming .... very slowly.
4. Do you know each ....?
5. Thanks for coming! Stay .... contact.

4 Match the beginnings of the sentences (1–5) with the endings (a–e).
1. Can you help me put — a your journey!
2. What time are you going to send — b this painting on the wall?
3. I hope you enjoy — c the documents to me?
4. Do you think he can repair — d all their stuff in this cupboard.
5. The children keep — e this table?

5 Complete the sentences with words formed from the words in brackets.
1. Did Malcolm find his .... cat? (lose)
2. I have a problem with my battery. Do you have your .... with you? (charge)
3. Are you ....? I can make you a sandwich. (hunger)
4. Take your map. It'll be very .... (use)
5. Yes. I'll .... call you when I get home. (definite)

Score ____/25

Wait a couple of weeks and try the quiz again.
Compare your scores.

AUDIOSCRIPT

Unit 1

🎧 1.1
three
five
six
nine
eleven
twelve

🎧 1.2
E = Ethan, I = Ines, K = Khalid
I: What's your name?
K: Khalid.
I: Hi. I'm Ines.
K: Nice to meet you.
I: Yes. You, too.
K: Ines, this is my friend Ethan.
I: Hi. Nice to meet you.
E: Yes. You, too, Ines.

🎧 1.3
H = Hugh, L = Liam, R= Rebeca, S = Shirley
1 S: Liam is my husband. He's a doctor.
2 L: Shirley is my wife. She's a teacher in an English school. This is my son, Hugh. He's nine. And she is my daughter, Rebeca. She's nine, too!
3 R: Hugh's my brother. He is my best friend, too. We're in the same class at school!
4 H: Rebeca is my sister. My mother is a teacher and my father is a doctor.

🎧 1.4
four
eight
twelve
fifteen
nineteen
twenty
twenty-two

🎧 1.5
1 thirty
2 eighteen
3 nineteen dollars ninety-nine
4 fourteen
5 seven euros fifty

🎧 1.6
A: What would you like?
B: How much is a small orange juice?
A: Three ninety-nine.
B: OK. A small orange juice, please.
A: Orange juice. Anything else?
B: Yes – a coffee cake, please.
A: OK. Anything else?
B: No, thanks.
A: That's seven ninety-nine.

🎧 1.7
A: Hi, what would you like, sir?
B: How much is a large latte?
A: Four fifty.
B: OK. A large latte, please.
A: Anything else?
B: Yes – a chocolate cake, please.
A: Thank you!
... Here you are. Is everything OK?
B: No. My latte – it's not right.
A: What's the problem, sir?
B: This is a small latte – not a large.
A: Oh, yes. Sorry. OK. That's nine ninety.

Unit 2

🎧 2.1
A = Angelina, S = Sebastian
S: Hi. Sorry. What's your name?
A: Angelina. And you?
S: Sebastian. Nice to meet you.
A: You, too.
S: So, Angelina. Where do you live?
A: I live on Venice Road. Do you know it?
S: Yes. It's near our school, right?
A: Yes. I walk here. It takes ten minutes.
S: Nice!
A: And you? Where do you live, Sebastian?
S: Westville. It's a small village. Do you know it?
A: No. Is it far?
S: It takes twenty minutes by bus.
A: Do you live in a house or a flat?
S: I live in a small flat with two friends. And you?
A: I live in a big house with my mother and father.

🎧 2.2
W= waiter, C1 = customer 1, C2 = customer 2
W: Are you ready to order?
C1: Yes. A burger with chips for me.
W: And you?
C2: The fish, please.
W: With rice or chips?
C2: Chips, please.
W: Anything else with your fish?
C2: How much is a salad?
W: It's ten pounds.
C2: Oh! No, thanks.

🎧 2.3
1
M = man, W = woman
M: I love espresso!
W: I don't like it. I only like tea.
2
B = boy, W = woman
B: I don't like vegetables, Mum!
W: Oh, Tommy! You only like cakes and ice cream!
B: I love cakes and ice cream!

3

M = man, W = waiter

M   Do you have a table for three?

W: Yes. Would you like a menu in English?

M: Yes, please.

4

M = man, W = waiter

W: Would you like a drink, sir?

M: How much is a coke?

W: Five euros thirty.

M: Oh. It's expensive. No, thanks.

2.4

bus driver

doctors

does

flats

hours

house

lives

south

Unit 3

3.1

1   an expensive flat

2   an orange bus

3   an English teacher

4   an old village

3.2

1

A: How's your son?

B: He's not very well.

A: Oh, no! I'm sorry.

B: How's your daughter?

A: She's great!

B: Good.

2

C: How's your flat?

D: It's good, but flats in the city are expensive.

C: Yes!

3

E: How's the weather?

F: It's very hot. I love it.

E: Oh. It's not normally hot in Canada.

4

G: How's your job?

H: It's not very good. How's *your* job?

G: The same. And it's difficult!

H: Yeah, I know.

3.3

B = Bandile, E = Emma

E: Where are you from, Bandile?

B: Buenos Aires.

E: Sorry? Can you say that again?

B: Buenos Aires, in Argentina.

E: Great. Welcome to London! Are you tired?

B: Sorry. Can you say that again?

E: Are you tired?

B: Er … yes. I'm hot and tired. I need to take a shower.

E: Oh, yes. Of course. Do you want anything?

B: Do you have … er, … for my shower …

E: A towel?

B: No, I have a towel. I need some … er, *seep*. How do you say *seep* in English?

E: Soap!

Unit 4

4.1

A: Is there a restaurant near here?

B: No, there isn't.

A: OK. Is there a café? I'm very hungry!

B: No, sorry, there isn't one on this road.

A: Oh. Is there a supermarket?

B: Yes, there's one next to the cinema! They have sandwiches.

4.2

1   A: Do you know a town called Southsea?

      B: No, is it far?

2   On Park Road, there's a clothes shop called Nice and New. I often go shopping there.

3   There's a nice restaurant called Angelo's near my house. It has great pizza!

4   A: There's a cinema called the Odeon there.

      B: Yes, do you want to see a film?

5   A: Do you know a café called The CoffeeShop?

      B: Yes, it's very expensive.

4.3

1

A: Excuse me. Do you know a café called the Big Cappuccino on this road?

B: Er … No, I don't. I don't know the town.

A: Oh, OK.

B: There are some cafés near here, but I don't know their names.

A: Oh.

B: Walk down this road. I think there's a café at the end.

A: Oh, yes – it is at the end of a road!

B: Maybe that's it. Down on the left; next to the park.

A: Yes, maybe. Thank you.

2

C: Hello. Excuse me.
D: Hello.
C: Is there a cash machine near here?
D: A cash machine ... No, there isn't a cash machine, but there's a bank on Maple Road. Down there. The first on the left.
C: Sorry, can you say that again?
D: Sorry. Down there. The first road. Go left.
C: The second road?
D: No, the first road. It's a big road called Maple Road. The bank is on the right.
C: Oh, great! Thank you!

3

E: Hello, excuse me. Excuse me.
F: Hi. Sorry. Yes.
E: Is there a swimming pool near here?
F: A swimming pool ... er... yes. There's one down there.
E: How far is it?
F: Er ... I don't know – 250 metres? It's near a hospital called St Ann's.
E: OK – near the hospital.
F: Yes – St Ann's is on the corner, on the right, and the swimming pool is on the left.
E: OK. Thanks.

⚇ 4.4

bank
station
hospital
market
supermarket
church

⚇ 4.5

station
hospital
market
supermarket

⚇ 4.6

1 A: Can you wait ten minutes?
   B: Sorry, I can't.
2 A: I don't know what floor my classroom is on. Can you help me?
   B: Sure!
3 A: This is difficult. Can we have a break?
   B: OK.
4 A: Do we have homework?
   B: Yes. Can you do Exercises 4 and 5?
5 A: We're cold.
   B: OK. Can you close the window?
6 A: Can we have food in the class?
   B: No, you can't.

UNIT 5

⚇ 5.1

J= Jason, W = Woman

W: Do you like my new flat, Jason?
J: Yes, it's great! Are there any interesting places near here?
W: Yes, there are lots of good places. You like museums. There are two interesting museums in this area.
J: Cool! And I want to go shopping. Are there any shops near here?
W: No, there are no shops, but there's a great market in the Old Town.
J: Is there a café in the Old Town?
W: Yes, there's a café called Coffee Express. It's really nice. Do you want to go there?
J: Yes, I need a coffee!

⚇ 5.2

1

A: Hello there. Are there any places to sit and have lunch near here?
B: Not on this road. There's a restaurant on North Road, but the best place is the Old Town. There are some good cafés there.
A: Great, thanks!

2

C: I want to go shopping this afternoon. Where's the best place to go?
D: Well, there's a supermarket in the city centre. It's about forty minutes from here. But there's a market here, in the village. It's very good. Lots of people go there.

3

E: Excuse me. I need to get some money. Are there any banks on this road?
F: No, there are no banks, but there's a cash machine. It's near the hospital.

4

G: Is there a good museum near here? I want to go somewhere interesting this afternoon.
H: Yes. There are lots of interesting places. Try the City Museum. It's on a street called Gosposka. Number 15.

5

I: I want to have a walk. Where's the best place to go?
J: Try the area round the Old Square. I walk there every day. There are lots of nice places to see and the main square is great.

⚇ 5.3

card
cash
centre
city
costs
first class
office
receipt

5.4

1
A: Where are you going?
B: To a town called Truro.
A: Oh. Is it far?

2
C: Where are you going?
D: To a city in France – Cannes.
C: Cool!

3
E: Where are you going?
F: To the Old Town – it's an interesting place.
E: Yes, I love it.

4
G: Where are you going?
H: To the main square. I want to sit and have a coffee.
G: Can I come?

5
I: Where are you going?
J: To Berlin.
I: Single or return?

Unit 6

6.1

1 A: Hi, Maria. Sorry, I'm late.
   B: That's OK. How was your journey?
2 A: I don't have any money for lunch.
   B: Don't worry. I have some.
3 A: Sorry, I'm late. I went to the wrong flat.
   B: That's OK. You're here now!
4 A: I can't come to the cinema. I had a problem at home.
   B: Don't worry. We can go tomorrow.
5 A: I don't have my English book.
   B: That's OK. You can share my book.

6.2

liked
rained
visited

6.3

danced
needed
shared
started
stayed
talked
walked
wanted
watched

6.4

C = Chang, M= Mia

M: Hi, Chang.
C: Hi, Mia. How are you?
M: Good, thanks.
C: Sorry, I'm late. I had a problem in the city. There was a lot of traffic in the centre.
M: That's OK – I know. It was on TV. How was work?
C: It wasn't very good. The shop was very busy, but there was no-one to help me.
M: Oh, I'm sorry. Are you hungry?
C: Yes, I didn't have lunch this afternoon. What are we doing this evening?
M: We're going to that restaurant on South Street.
C: Oh. I didn't like that restaurant. It wasn't very big and there were a lot of people there.
M: Don't worry. Do you want to stay at home?
C: Is that OK? I did a lot of work today and I'm tired.
M: Of course! I can get a pizza.
C: OK, good. Sorry, Mia. I went to bed late last night. I want to go to bed early tonight.

Unit 7

7.1

1

T= Tomas, W= woman

W: Hi, Tomas. How are you? Did you have a good weekend? What did you do?
T: Not much. I stayed in my flat and read.
W: Do you read a lot?
T: Yes.
W: Me, too. What do you like reading?
T: Books, usually. And you?
W: I prefer magazines, but I read *The Year of the Flood* and I really liked that.
T: Really? I read it, but I didn't like it. I prefer *The Handmaid's Tale*. That's my favourite book.

2

A= Akeno, W= woman

W: Hey, Akeno. Did you go out yesterday?
A: Yes, I went to the gym with my friend, Hans.
W: Do you do a lot of exercise?
A: Yes. I usually go running every evening and I often play football on Sunday afternoons. Do you like doing exercise?
W: Not really, I prefer listening to music. But I like dancing.
A: Do you have a favourite singer?
W: Yes, Tae-yeon. She's a great singer!
A: Oh, right, I don't know her. Do you have a favourite band?
W: Rainbow!
A: Rainbow from the UK or Rainbow from South Korea?
W: South Korea, of course!
A: I prefer Rainbow from the UK. They're an old band, but they're great!

3

J= Joseph, W= woman

W: Hello, Joseph. What did you do yesterday?

J: I stayed at home and watched TV.

W: Oh. Did you watch anything good?

J: Yes, a programme called *Father Brown* – I love it.

W: Yes, me, too. What else do you watch on TV?

J: Different series from the UK. Sometimes I watch programmes about travel.

W: OK. Do you have a favourite series?

J: Not really. I love everything English.

W: Right.

7.2

American

Brazilian

Egyptian

Italian

Mexican

Russian

7.3

1   A: What do you think of this skirt?

    B: It's OK, but it's a bit long.

2   A: Look at this shirt. What do you think?

    B: Sorry. I don't really like it.

3   A: What do you think of these jeans?

    B: They're OK, but I'm not sure about the design.

4   A: What do you think of the jumper?

    B: I really like it! It looks great!

5   A: What do you think of the trainers?

    B: They're nice, but I'm not sure about the price.

Unit 8

8.1

1

B = Becky, F= Fran

F: But my son said ... Oh, sorry, Becky. I need to answer this.

B: That's OK, Fran.

F: Thanks. Hello? Oh, hi, David. How're you? ...
Oh, OK. Don't worry. ...
OK. Thank you for calling. Have a good trip. Bye.
Right ... sorry.

B: That's OK. Was that your brother?

F: No, a client. He's flying to Rome today, so he can't come to our meeting tomorrow.

B: Oh. Why is he going to Rome then?

F: There's a problem in their Italian office. It's OK, he wants to meet on Friday now.

B: Oh, really? Can you do that?

F: Well, I can, but ... .

B: Is there a problem?

F: I'm going to meet another client in the morning.

B: What time does your client want to meet on Friday?

F: Three o'clock in the afternoon – I can do that. But I'm going to have a busy day!

2

A: How's your brother? Is he OK?

B: John? He's great. He's working at a school in the US now.

A: Oh, really? Is he a teacher?

B: Yes, he's a Spanish teacher.

A: Oh. That's a good job.

B: Yes. He's making a lot of money and he loves the US.

A: Oh, good.

B: I'm going to visit him next week.

A: Oh great, say hello.

3

A = Adam, E = Emma, J = Joseph, P = Poppy, S = Sofia,

E: Hi, Poppy. Where is everyone? It's seven twenty now, and the film starts at seven thirty.

P: Don't worry. They're coming. Look, here's Joseph.

J: Hello! Where's Adam? And where's Sofia?

P: Hi, Joseph. It's OK, they're coming. Adam's on the train now and Sofia is walking here from the station.

E: Oh. Here's Sofia. ... Why didn't you take a taxi?

S: It's a really nice evening – I wanted to walk. And it isn't far from the station.

P: Oh, look! There's Adam.

A: Sorry, I'm a bit late.

E: Don't worry. We can get the tickets now.

8.2

getting

making

meeting

studying

taking

travelling

working

8.3

1   A: Where did you last see your tablet?

    B: I can't remember. Maybe on the train.

2   A: When did you last see your friend, Suli?

    B: I'm not sure. Maybe Saturday night.

3   A: How far is your university from here?

    B: I don't know – not far. Maybe a ten-minute walk.

4   A: Where's Kim today?

    B: I'm not sure. Maybe she's at home.

5   A: What time were you in the café?

    B: I'm not sure. Maybe at two o'clock.

8.4

designer

good

manager

8.5

Argentina
change
daughter
get
glasses
green
gym
high
sign

8.6

1 I'm sorry. I don't know the answer.
2 My wife has a business – a lot of people work there.
3 Can you guess what's in that cupboard?
4 What does it say on that sign?
5 Are you writing an email to your mum?
6 I can climb that high mountain!

UNIT 9

9.1

1

J = John, P = Pam

J: Hello, Pam! How was your holiday?
P: Great! I went to the Philippines.
J: I went there a few months ago. It was nice, but I ate some fish and I felt really sick.
P: Oh, no!

2

C = Chan, L = Lee

L: Hi, Chan. I didn't see you at the gym last Friday.
C: Hello, Lee. No, I had a bad cold. I didn't go out last week.
L: Are you feeling better?
C: Oh, yes. Much better, thanks.

3

I = Ivan, R = Rob, S = Steven

R: Steven, this is Ivan.
S: Hi, Ivan.
I: Hi, Steven. I think I know you! You work in the local bank.
S: No, I worked in the bank before, but I hurt my back three years ago. Now, I work at home.
I: Oh, I'm sorry!
S: That's OK. My back's OK now, and I love my new job!

4

D = Dylan, L = Lin

D: Hi, Lin. Are you feeling OK?
L: Hi, Dylan. Yes, I'm fine, but my husband, Joe, was in hospital.
D: Oh no! What happened?
L: He was in the kitchen and he broke something – a dish – and he cut his hand.
D: When was that?
L: This morning.

9.2

A B C D E F G H I J K L M N O P Q R S T U V W X Y Z

9.3

A E I O U

9.4

conversation
safe
back
hand
cold
broke
doctor
hospital

UNIT 10

10.1

M = Miguel, C = Carol

M: Hi, Carol. Come in. ... Oh, no! You're wet. Do you want a towel?
C: No, don't worry, Miguel, thanks. Oh, I hate the rain! Is it going to stay like this?
M: No, I don't think so. I think the weather's going to change. Why? Do you have plans?
C: Yes, I'm going into Madrid to go shopping tomorrow, and I hate driving in the rain.
M: Me too. I hate the winter when it's like this. I talked to my Australian friend, Loretta, today. It's summer in Australia now. It's 35 degrees in Melbourne and she's going to have a barbecue with some friends!
C: Nice! I got an email from my brother, James, this morning. It's wet and windy everywhere in England today – it's like here in Spain.
M: Is it cold there now?
C: Yes, I think so. James wrote that he's going to make dinner for some friends this evening and they're going to eat in front of the fire.
M: It's very cold in Canada now, too. My friend, Lucas, is working in Montreal. I talked to him last night. There's lots of snow there, and he's going skiing in the mountains on Sunday.
C: Really? I love skiing.
M: I prefer summer sports – swimming at the beach is my favourite.
C: Well, we can't swim at the beach now!
M: No, but we can go to a pool. My gym has a pool, and I'm going swimming tomorrow afternoon.

10.2

1

A = Ava, T = Thomas

A: Do you have plans for the weekend, Thomas?
T: No, nothing special. And you?
A: No, I don't have any plans. Do you want to go somewhere and listen to some music?
T: Yeah, great.
A: How about a club? Glorious Sons are playing at Club 22 tonight.
T: I don't really like clubs. I'd prefer a concert in the park.

2

A = Alan, M = Meghan

A: Are you doing anything on Saturday, Meghan?
M: No, I don't think so. Do you want to do something together?
A: OK. How about a classical concert?
M: I don't really like classical concerts. I'd prefer a comedy show. There's one at the café on Maple Street on Saturday night.
A: OK. I'm going shopping at five. I'll meet you after that.

⚫ **10.3**
club
he
help
June
meet
music
spend
sun

Unit 11

⚫ **11.1**

1 A: We're having a barbecue on Saturday. Can you and your wife come?
B: Maybe. I need to check. Can I call you later?
A: OK.

2 A: I've finished my exams, so I'm going to have a party. Do you want to come?
B: I'd love to. What day?
A: Saturday.
B: Oh, no. Sorry, I can't. I'm going away for work.
A: OK.

3 A: I need a weekend away, so I'm going camping. Do you want to come?
B: Sure. What dates?
A: The fifth and sixth.
B: Great!

4 A: There's a conference in Madrid next week. Can you come?
B: Maybe. What day?
A: Next Friday.
B: OK, I think so, but I need to check my diary.

⚫ **11.2**

T = Tonya, A = Ali

T: Hi, Ali. Did you know today's the first of September?
A: What? Already? Where did the summer go?
T: Yes, I know. Oh, well. I like September – it's not hot.
A: Me, too. It's my birthday in the second week of September. I'm going to have a party at Luigi's, the Italian restaurant on South Street. Do you want to come?
T: Sure. I'd love to. That's a great restaurant. What date?
A: The ninth.
T: I think that's OK, but I need to check my diary. Can I tell you later?
A: Sure.
T: OK, good. I'm celebrating this month, too. I married Larry ten years ago. It's our anniversary!
A: Oh, nice. When is it?

T: It's in the middle of September – on the twentieth.
A: Are you and Larry going anywhere to celebrate?
T: No, we're going to stay at home and have a big barbecue. Lots of our friends are coming. Can you come?
A: Maybe. What day?
T: Saturday – in the afternoon – at three.
A: Sure! I can come. What's your address?
T: Fourteen New Road.
A: Great, thanks.
T: And after that, it's that conference in Tokyo at the end of September.
A: That's right! What dates?
T: We're going on the 26th and back on the 29th.
A: Is your boss coming?
T: Yes, she's coming, too. But she's coming on the 27th.
A: Oh, OK.

⚫ **11.3**
busy
died
history
hungry
night
outside
prison
why
with

Unit 12

⚫ **12.1**
1

M = Mike, S = Soraya

M: Oh, this coffee is very nice. How's your cappuccino, Soraya?
S: I don't like it. It's very strong!
M: Oh, no. I'll go and get you another one.
S: Are you sure?
M: Yes, it's fine. I want to order another cake, too. …
S: Oh, that's great, thanks for that! Oh! You didn't get a cake!
M: No, there are no cakes! Well, there are cakes, but no chocolate ones.
S: Here! You can have mine – I'm full.
M: Really? Are you sure?
S: Yeah, it's fine.
M: OK. Thanks, Soraya.

2

M = man, W = woman

M: My burger and chips were good. How was the chicken?

W: Really good. They have great food here. ...
    Oh, no. My phone's not working! The battery's low and I
    really need to talk to a client. He wanted to see me.

M: Don't worry. I'll lend you mine, if you like.

W: OK. Thanks. I'll go and call him.
    ...
    So, my client wants to meet at two o'clock.

M: Two o'clock today? It's one o'clock now!

W: I know! And the meeting's in the city centre. There's a lot of
    traffic – I'm going to be late!

M: Don't worry. I'll take you if you want.

W: Really? Are you sure?

M: Yeah, it's fine!

W: That's great. Thanks. I'll buy lunch.

M: OK!

⬤ 12.2

back

chocolate

computer

contact

get

home

hope

me

place

safe

send

stuff

sunny

taxi

rule

we

ANSWER KEY

UNIT 1

VOCABULARY Numbers 1–12

1

G	J	T	F	I	V	E	U	J	G
G	S	W	E	E	T	J	S	X	I
A	B	E	J	Y	H	E	E	S	S
G	F	L	Q	K	R	K	L	T	I
O	V	V	K	S	E	V	E	N	X
D	F	E	H	O	E	F	V	W	T
G	T	W	O	O	N	E	E	I	E
T	C	Z	N	B	N	I	N	E	N
J	F	O	U	R	E	I	G	H	T
A	E	Y	X	K	R	H	G	C	Z

2
Students should circle: 3, 5, 6, 9, 11, 12

LISTENING

3
Picture 2

4

Ines, this is my friend Ethan.	6
Hi. I'm Ines.	3
Hi. Nice to meet you.	7
Khalid.	2
Nice to meet you.	4
What's your name?	1
Yes. You, too, Ines.	8
Yes. You, too.	5

DEVELOPING CONVERSATIONS Checking names

5
1 he   2 She's   3 they   4 I

6
1 I   3 's he   5 know
2 's she   4 are they   6 Who

VOCABULARY People

7
1 doctor   3 friend   5 mother
2 teacher   4 son   6 wife

8
1 father   3 brother   5 sister
2 daughter   4 husband

9
1 husband   3 brother, friend
2 teacher, daughter   4 mother, father

GRAMMAR 'm, 's, 're

10
1 's   2 'm   3 's   4 's   5 're   6 is   7 're   8 're

11
1 We're   2 He's   3 She's   4 I'm   5 They're

VOCABULARY Numbers 13–22

1
18 15 21 4 17 22 13 16
14 3 10 12 19 8 20 9

3
wz fourteen zst eighteen hj twenty ox thirteen vx fifteen uh seventeen mn twenty-two vu sixteen op nineteen nh twenty-one

VOCABULARY Question words

4
1 What time   3 How much   5 Where
2 How old   4 Who   6 How long

5
1 Where   3 How long   5 How old
2 What time   4 How much   6 Who

GRAMMAR Questions with *be*

6
1 are   3 is   5 Are   7 is
2 is   4 is   6 are   8 Are

7
1 What time is the break?   5 Who is he?
2 How much are the books?   6 Where is Akemi from?
3 How are you?   7 How old is Ava?
4 Is the coffee nice?   8 How long are the classes?

8
a 8   b 4   c 5   d 6   e 1   f 2   g 3   h 7

GRAMMAR *his, her, our, their*

9
1 c   2 b   3 a   4 d

10
1 our   2 his   3 their   4 her

11
1 her   3 their   5 our
2 Ethan's   4 Sharon's

READING

12
1 c   2 a   3 b

13
1 T   2 F   3 F   4 T   5 F   6 T

14
1 How long; three hours
2 What; 4pm–7pm
3 What; Friday
4 Who; Morgan and Sian's older son
5 How; She's 21.
6 Where's; a restaurant / Sam's Restaurant / 18 Brown Street

VOCABULARY Times and prices

1

eighty	forty	thirty-two
fifty-seven	seventy	twenty
ninety-six	sixty-three	

2
1 T   2 P   3 P   4 T   5 T   6 P

PRONUNCIATION Numbers

3

1 b   2 b   3 a   4 a   5 b

VOCABULARY In a coffee shop

5

1	sandwich	3	tea	5	large
2	cake	4	small		

DEVELOPING CONVERSATIONS Ordering and serving drinks

6

1	would	3	much	5	Anything
2	like	4	else	6	thanks

GRAMMAR *not*

8

1 My sandwich – it's **not** right.
2 It's **not** a chocolate cake.
3 It's small – **not** medium.
4 My cappuccino – it's **not** hot.
5 A latte is $3.69 – **not** $5.69!

9

1 It's not right.   4 It's not five pounds.
2 It's not small.   5 My americano is not hot.
3 It's not a coffee cake.

LISTENING

10

b

11

1	Hi	3	Four fifty	5	large
2	latte	4	small	6	nine ninety

12

2 and 4

DEVELOPING WRITING Describing people

13

1 **C**ome to our party at 3 **H**igh **S**treet.
2 **T**his is my daughter, **P**oppy.
3 **H**i, I'm **L**ara.
4 **H**e's from **S**ão **P**aulo in **B**razil.
5 **T**his is our son, **D**avid.

14

1, 3, 5, 6, 7, 8

VOCABULARY BUILDER QUIZ 1

1

1 D   2 F   3 F   4 D   5 F   6 D   7 D

2

1	wife	3	invitation	5	Sunday
2	daughter	4	brother	6	school

3

1	flat	3	know	5	meet
2	right	4	name	6	juice

4

1	from	3	friend	5	**A**nything
2	cl**a**ss	4	br**ea**k	6	m**e**di**u**m

UNIT 2

VOCABULARY My home

1

hn(centre)cdki(city)pl(flats)qw(house)br(north)ol(road)dw(south)
ky(park)mn(village)as

2

1	village	4	house	7	park
2	north	5	road	8	flats
3	south	6	city		

GRAMMAR Present simple

3

1	walk	3	live	5	have	7	knows
2	takes	4	has	6	like		

4

1	knows	3	know	5	have	7	lives
2	live	4	like	6	takes		

5

1	like	3	have	5	likes
2	has	4	lives	6	knows

GRAMMAR Present simple questions: *do you … ?*

6

1	Do you like	3	Do you have	5	Do you know
2	Who do you live	4	Where do you	6	Do you walk

7

a 3   b 2   c 5   d 4   e 6   f 1

8

1 Do you live with your mother and father?
2 Do you like my husband's village?
3 Do you have a big house?
4 Where do you live?
5 Who do you know here?
6 Where do you have a flat?

DEVELOPING CONVERSATIONS *And you?*

9

1	I'm twenty. And you?	2
	I'm eighteen.	3
	How old are you?	1
2	I'm great.	3
	Fine, thanks. And you?	2
	How are you?	1
3	Caleb. And you?	2
	Marianna.	3
	What's your name?	1

10

1	I'm OK.	3	Near the park.	5	No, it's very big.
2	Suki.	4	Yes, a sister.		

LISTENING

11

1, 4, 6, 7

12

1	on Venice Road	3	walks	5	small
2	their school	4	a flat	6	friends

VOCABULARY Jobs

1
1 bus driver, a
2 mum, d
3 nurse, h
4 retired, f
5 student, g
6 teacher, b
7 waiter, c
8 work in an office, e

GRAMMAR Present simple: *don't (do not)*

2
1 I don't live in a flat.
2 They don't like big cities.
3 We don't go to school.
4 You don't have a job.
5 They don't work in an office.

3
Students' own answers

GRAMMAR Plural / no plural

4
✓ 1, 2, 5, 8, 9
✗ 3, 4, 6, 7

5
1 nurses
2 children
3 students
4 ✗
5 people
6 flats
7 ✗
8 drinks
9 mums
10 areas

6
1 is
2 time
3 are
4 houses
5 are
6 flats

READING

7
1 Canada
2 England
3 Sweden
4 Poland

8
1 F 2 T 3 F 4 T 5 F 6 F 7 T 8 F

DEVELOPING WRITING Writing a description of yourself

9
1 a 2 c 3 d 4 b 5 e 6 g 7 f

10
1 Acacia Gonzales
2 19
3 Mexico
4 Comitán
5 Chiapas
6 south
7 my mother and father
8 Instituto Tecnológico

11
Students' own answers

VOCABULARY Food and drinks

1
1 orange juice
2 salad
3 drinks
4 coffee cake
5 meat

2
Across
1 juice
3 fish
5 meat
Down
2 chicken
3 fruit
4 salad

GRAMMAR *like / don't like*

3
1 don't like
2 love
3 like
4 don't like
5 like
6 love

4
Students' own answers

5
1 it
2 them
3 them
4 it
5 it
6 them

DEVELOPING CONVERSATIONS Ordering food

6
1 Anything else with your fish?   W
2 Are you ready to order?   W
3 Chips, please.   C
4 The fish, please.   C
5 How much is a salad?   C
6 And you?   W
7 It's ten pounds.   W
8 Oh! No, thanks.   C
9 With rice or chips?   W
10 Yes. A burger with chips for me.   C

7
W: Are you ready to order?
C: Yes. A burger with chips for me.
W: And you?
C: The fish, please.
W: With rice or chips?
C: Chips, please.
W: Anything else with your fish?
C: How much is a salad?
W: It's ten pounds.
C: Oh! No, thanks.

LISTENING

9
1 b 2 d 3 c 4 a

10
1 F 2 T 3 T 4 T 5 F 6 F 7 F 8 T

PRONUNCIATION /z/ and /s/

11
/z/ and /s/

12
/z/: doctors, does, hours, lives
/s/: bus driver, flats, house, south

VOCABULARY BUILDER QUIZ 2

1
1 PL 2 PL 3 P 4 P 5 PL 6 P 7 P

2
1 expensive
2 person
3 carrot
4 ice cream
5 minute
6 dog

3
1 vegetables
2 south
3 dad
4 small
5 far
6 chips

4
1 live
2 hours
3 area
4 house
5 retired
6 university

UNIT 3

VOCABULARY Adjectives

1
1 d   2 b   3 a   4 c

2
1 difficult   4 hungry   7 tired
2 expensive   5 married   8 well
3 great   6 nice

3
1 a, hot   3 an, old   5 an, expensive
2 a, big   4 a, hungry   6 a, tired

PRONUNCIATION Saying words together

4
1 an expensive   3 an English
2 an orange   4 an old

GRAMMAR Negatives with *be*

6
1 's not   3 're not   5 's not
2 're not   4 'm not

7
1 's not   3 's not   5 'm not
2 're not   4 're not

8
1 's not   2 're not   3 're not   4 's not   5 'm not

LISTENING

9
1 c   2 d   3 a   4 b

10
a 3   b 1   c 4   d 2

11
1 very well   3 hot
2 expensive   4 very good, difficult

DEVELOPING CONVERSATIONS Responding to news

13
Good news: She's very well, thanks. It's very nice. The other
            students are great.
Bad news: It's very cold here. My chicken's not hot. His job is
            difficult.

14
1 It's very cold here.   4 My chicken's not hot.
2 His job is difficult.   5 The other students are great.
3 She's very well, thanks.   6 It's very nice.

15
1 I'm sorry.   3 Oh, good.   5 Oh, good.
2 I'm sorry.   4 I'm sorry.   6 Oh, good.

VOCABULARY *go, take, want*

1
1 takes   3 wants   5 takes   7 takes
2 goes   4 goes   6 wants

2
1 takes   5 goes   9 goes
2 goes   6 wants   10 goes
3 takes   7 goes   11 takes
4 takes   8 wants

GRAMMAR Present simple: *doesn't*

3
1 He doesn't like fish.
2 Leo doesn't know my teacher.
3 The train doesn't take a long time.
4 My brother doesn't want to go to the party.
5 The bus doesn't go to the city.
6 She doesn't live in a new house.

4
1 She doesn't take the train.
2 He doesn't like his hotel.
3 Maria doesn't go shopping every day.
4 My mother doesn't have a car.
5 It doesn't take long to walk to school.
6 The number 10 bus doesn't go near my gym.

5
1 wants, doesn't want   3 takes, doesn't like
2 has, doesn't have   4 takes, doesn't take

GRAMMAR Present simple questions: *does*

6
1 f   2 c   3 d   4 a   5 b   6 e

7
1 Why   3 How   5 What
2 Where   4 What   6 Who

8
1 How long does the bus take?
2 What does your brother do?
3 Where does Steven work?
4 When does she go to the gym?
5 Where does he go at two o'clock?

READING

9
Lucia and Vincenzo

10
1 Does   4 Does   7 Is
2 What   5 Does   8 Does
3 Where   6 How much

11
1 a   2 b   3 a   4 b   5 b   6 b   7 a   8 a

VOCABULARY Things

1
Across
2 food   4 map   6 towel   7 shoes   8 coat
Down
1 soap   3 dictionary   5 pen

2
1 map   2 pen   3 money   4 brush   5 food

DEVELOPING CONVERSATIONS Asking for help in conversation

3

1	Sorry	3	Can	5	How
2	say	4	again	6	English

GRAMMAR *a* and *any*

5

Do you have a ...?: book, brush, coat, map, mobile
Do you have any ...?: bags, food, local money, other shoes,
    toothpaste

6

1	any	4	anything	7	any	10	any
2	anything	5	a	8	any	11	any
3	any	6	a	9	any		

7

Students' own answers

DEVELOPING WRITING Writing an email

8

1 b   2 a

9

1 b   2 d   3 f   4 a   5 c   6 g   7 e

10

Students' own answers

VOCABULARY BUILDER QUIZ 3

1

1	a book	3	shopping	5	married
2	clothes	4	a shower	6	holiday

2

1	room	3	phone	5	charger
2	time	4	paste	6	time

3

1	very	3	difficult	5	local	7	adjectives
2	hungry	4	other	6	expensive		

4

1 b   2 e   3 d   4 f   5 c   6 a

UNIT 4

VOCABULARY Places

1

1	pool	3	station	5	market
2	machine	4	park	6	shop

2

1	church	4	restaurant	7	cinema		
2	café	5	park	8	hotel		
3	hospital	6	bank	9	market		

3

1	church	5	hotel	9	restaurant
2	supermarket	6	cinema	10	car park
3	café	7	bank		
4	hospital	8	park		

GRAMMAR *Is there ... ? / There's ...*

4

1	Is there	4	There's	7	There's
2	There's	5	there isn't	8	Is there
3	there isn't	6	Is there		

5

1	Is there	3	Is there	5	Is there
2	there isn't	4	there isn't	6	there's

VOCABULARY EXTRA Prepositions and directions

7

1	on	4	at the end	7	down
2	next to	5	near	8	on the left
3	in	6	on the corner		

8

1	down	3	near	5	in	7	on
2	next	4	on	6	at	8	right

DEVELOPING CONVERSATIONS *called*

9

1	town	3	restaurant	5	café
2	clothes shop	4	cinema		

LISTENING

10

1 c   2 b   3 a

11

1 e   2 d   3 b   4 f   5 c   6 a

PRONUNCIATION Syllable stress

1

1	1 syllable	3	3 syllables	5	4 syllables
2	2 syllables	4	2 syllables	6	1 syllable

2

1	<u>sta</u>tion	3	<u>mar</u>ket
2	<u>hos</u>pital	4	<u>super</u>market

VOCABULARY Days and times of day

3

1	Sunday	4	Wednesday	7	Saturday
2	Monday	5	Thursday		
3	Tuesday	6	Friday		

4

1	night	3	yesterday	5	tomorrow
2	afternoon	4	today		

5

1	morning	3	afternoon	5	night
2	from	4	evening	6	to

6

1 Tuesday
2 Today: Saturday   Yesterday: Friday
3 Tomorrow: Wednesday   Yesterday: Monday

GRAMMAR Adverbs of frequency

7

100%	always
75%	normally / usually
25%	sometimes
0%	never

8

1	always	4	usually / normally
2	sometimes	5	usually / normally
3	never		

9

Students' own answers

Reading

10

b

11

1 usually   2 always   3 normally   4 always

12

1 She's from Nova Scotia, Canada.
2 She's a teacher.
3 In a school (in a small village).
4 In the city. / At a supermarket called Sobey's and clothes shop called Winners.
5 At 4 (in the afternoon).
6 Fresh fruit.
7 Her friends.
8 Her job.
9 Weekends.

Grammar *Can ...?*

1

a 5   b 4   c 6   d 1   e 3   f 2

2

1 Can I   3 Can you   5 Can you
2 Can you   4 Can I   6 Can I

3

1 Can we have a break?
2 Can we have ten more minutes?
3 Can we have food in the class?
4 Can you close the window?
5 Can you do Exercise 9?
6 Can you help me?
7 Can you wait a minute?

Vocabulary Classroom verbs

4

1 c   2 f   3 e   4 d/h   5 b   6 a   7 d/h   8 g

5

1 leave   3 Come   5 Use
2 Turn on   4 write   6 share

Developing Writing A note describing where you live

6

1 but   2 but   3 and   4 and   5 but   6 and

7

1 c   2 b

8

1 20 Garden Road   4 at 10 in the morning
2 take the train   5 down the road
3 museum there called

9

Students' own answers

10

Students' own answers

Vocabulary Builder Quiz 4

1

1 a film   3 a shop   5 your tablet
2 $5   4 English

2

1 machine   3 shop   5 name
2 station   4 park

3

1 b   2 d   3 a   4 c   5 e

4

1 third   3 evening   5 today
2 mosque   4 book

5

1 many   3 called   5 understand
2 right   4 closed

UNIT 5

Vocabulary Getting there

1

get: a taxi, home, off the train, the metro, the red line, to work
go: home, to work
take: a taxi, the metro, the red line
walk: home, to work
change: trains
wait: for the bus

2

1 get, walk   3 go   5 get
2 Take, change   4 wait, take

Grammar Are there ... ? / There are ...

3

1 c   2 a   3 b   4 c   5 b   6 a   7 b   8 b

5

1 Are there   3 There's   5 There are
2 a   4 Is there a   6 any

6

Students' own answers

7

Students' own answers

Developing Conversations *best*

8

1 It's far from here. It's best to take a taxi.
2 Where's the best place to see some interesting art?
3 What's the best area in the city?
4 Is that the best café to sit and have a coffee?
5 Where's the best place to go swimming?

Listening

9

1 b   2 e   3 c   4 a   5 d

10

1 T   2 F   3 F   4 T   5 F   6 T   7 T   8 F
9 T   10 F

Vocabulary Buying tickets

1

1 change trains
2 pay by card
3 first class
4 the next train
5 return
6 second class
7 single

2

Across
2 card   4 machine   5 cash
Down
1 ticket   3 receipt

3

1 change   4 machine   7 next
2 pay, card   5 enter   8 receipt
3 first class   6 return

Pronunciation /k/ and /s/

4

/k/ and /s/

5

/k/: card, cash, costs, first class
/s/: centre, city, office, receipt

Reading

7

Advert 2

8

1 a   2 a   3 b   4 a   5 b   6 a

Developing Conversations *Where are you going?*

10

Conversation 1: d   Conversation 4: b
Conversation 2: a   Conversation 5: c
Conversation 3: e

Grammar Talking about plans: *I'm / We're going*

1

Where: to the bank, to the market, to the museum, home
What: to see some interesting art, to go swimming
When: this evening, now

2

1 I'm going   3 're going   5 'm going
2 're going   4 'm going   6 're going

3

1 'm going to play   4 're going to see
2 're going to have   5 'm going to eat
3 'm going to meet   6 're going to stay

4

Students' own answers

Grammar Asking about plans: *going* and *doing*

5

1 going   2 going   3 doing   4 going   5 doing

6

1 Where are you going   3 Are you going
2 What time are you going   4 What are you doing

Developing Writing Writing a text message

7

1 He   2 It's   3 She's   4 They

8

1 She   2 He   3 They   4 It

9

b

10

1 tonight   3 *Deadpool 2*   5 eight
2 the cinema   4 the metro

11

Students' own answers

12

Students' own answers

Vocabulary Builder Quiz 5

1

1 o'clock   3 cash   5 passengers
2 outside   4 main

2

1 flight   3 return   5 views
2 line   4 journey

3

1 every   3 a long time   5 some help
2 second class   4 work

4

1 home   3 football   5 platform
2 card   4 museum

5

1 d   2 c   3 a   4 b   5 e

UNIT 6
Vocabulary Problems

1

1 late   3 rain   5 tired
2 noise   4 no-one   6 traffic

2

1 wrong   4 rain   7 late
2 traffic   5 no-one   8 nowhere
3 noise   6 tired   9 a problem

Grammar Past simple: irregular verbs

3

1 was   3 had   5 did
2 were   4 went

4

1 were   4 was   7 did
2 had   5 was, did, went
3 went   6 was

Developing Conversations *Don't worry / That's OK*

5

1 That   3 OK   5 That's
2 Don't   4 worry

READING

6
b

7
1 T 2 F 3 T 4 T 5 F 6 F

8
1 Turkey
2 six hours and thirty minutes
3 Via Laietana
4 La Rambla
5 evening

VOCABULARY Hotels and checking in

1
1	check out	4	breakfast	7 password
2	bag	5	key	8 passport
3	room	6	lift	

1 check out   4 breakfast   7 password
2 bag   5 key   8 passport
3 room   6 lift

2
1 address, number   5 lift
2 passport   6 booking
3 breakfast, check out 7 password
4 key   8 bag

GRAMMAR Regular past simple endings

3
verb + -d: liked, loved, shared
verb + -ed: rained, stayed, talked

4
1 liked   3 rained   5 talked
2 stayed   4 loved   6 shared

PRONUNCIATION Past simple forms

5
different
/t/: liked
/d/: rained
/id/: visited

6
/t/: talked, walked, watched
/d/: danced, shared, stayed
/id/: needed, started, wanted

GRAMMAR Past simple negatives

8
1 didn't have   4 didn't see   7 didn't go
2 didn't like   5 didn't talk 8 weren't
3 didn't rain   6 wasn't   9 didn't

9
1 It didn't rain in my city on Friday.
2 On my trip, I didn't see interesting art.
3 At school, I didn't talk to my English teacher.
4 I didn't have a party last weekend.
5 On my holiday, I didn't like the local food.
6 I didn't do a lot of work today.
7 On my bus journey, there wasn't a lot of noise.
8 I didn't go shopping yesterday.

10
Students' own answers

LISTENING

11
3

12
1 f   2 b   3 h   4 a   5 d   6 i   7 c
8 g   9 e

GRAMMAR Past simple questions

1
1 did you have   4 did you see   7 did you do
2 did you go   5 did you get   8 Did you go
3 did you leave 6 Did you go

2
Students' own answers

3
1 did you buy, c   4 did you get up, e
2 did you live, a   5 did you study, f
3 did you go, d   6 Did you stay, b

GRAMMAR REVIEW: Past simple

4
1 There was a problem at the café.
2 We weren't late for class.
3 I had breakfast at home.
4 They didn't go to the museum.
5 We did a lot of interesting things.
6 When did you get home?
7 I didn't like Rome.
8 We stayed in a great hostel.
9 Did you talk to the doctor? / Did the doctor talk to you?
10 Where did you have dinner?

5
1 was
2 went
3 did you have, didn't have, was
4 did you stay, stayed
5 was, weren't
6 Did you like, shared
7 did you see, didn't go, walked

DEVELOPING WRITING Writing a review

6
1 to   3 were   5 We're
2 their   4 two   6 there

7
b

8
Students' own answers

9
Students' own answers

VOCABULARY BUILDER QUIZ 6

1
1 music   3 flight   5 tour
2 no-one   4 password

2
1 traffic   3 booking   5 key
2 hungry   4 band

3

1	party	3	exercise	5	problem
2	your bed	4	weather		

4

1	passport	3	lake	5	lift
2	star	4	rain		

5

1 b   2 d   3 a   4 e   5 c

UNIT 7

VOCABULARY Words for activities

1

cook: Italian food
do: some exercise
go: on the internet, running, shopping, to concerts
read: a magazine, stories
listen: to a band, to a song
watch: a football game, a series on TV, videos

2

1 d   2 f   3 a   4 b   5 e   6 g   7 c

GRAMMAR *like + -ing*

3

1	Do you like living	4	likes
2	doesn't like, Do you like	5	don't like cleaning
3	love going	6	loves

4

1	playing	3	✓	5	visiting	7	going
2	✓	4	staying	6	✓		

5

1 I don't like driving in the city.
2 They like watching programmes about modern art.
3 We love doing exercise at the gym.
4 Do you like swimming in the sea?
5 Peter doesn't like looking at Facebook.
6 Danielle loves cooking Chinese food.

DEVELOPING CONVERSATIONS *Me too* and *I prefer*

6

1 D   2 S   3 D   4 S   5 S

7

Students' own answers

LISTENING

8

1 b   2 c   3 a

9

1 F   2 T   3 F   4 F   5 F   6 T   7 F
8 T   9 T

VOCABULARY Country adjectives

1

1	Brazilian	5	Japanese	9	Spanish
2	Chinese	6	Mexican	10	British
3	Egyptian	7	Polish	11	American
4	Italian	8	Russian		

2

1	American	4	Spanish	7	Mexican
2	Russian	5	Japanese	8	Egyptian
3	British	6	Brazilian		

PRONUNCIATION /ən/, /iən/ and /ʃən/

3

ən, iən and ʃən

4

ən: American, Mexican
iən: Brazilian, Italian
ʃən: Egyptian, Russian

GRAMMAR Present continuous (*I'm* and *are you ...?*)

6

1	'm listening to	5	'm looking at
2	'm making	6	Are you reading
3	Are you playing	7	are you doing
4	'm doing		

7

1 b   2 a   3 b   4 a   5 a

READING

8

1 c   2 a   3 b

9

1 S   2 C   3 H   4 C   5 H   6 S   7 C   8 S

10

1 F   2 F   3 F   4 T   5 T   6 F

GRAMMAR *this/these, one/ones*

1

1 a, c   2 a, b   3 a, d   4 b, d

2

1	this	3	This	5	These	7	ones
2	one	4	one	6	ones	8	ones

VOCABULARY Buying clothes

3

1	green, percent	4	dress, design
2	blue, brown	5	extra large
3	coat, comfortable		

4

1	jacket	4	half	7	long
2	white	5	jeans, T-shirts		
3	yellow	6	good		

DEVELOPING CONVERSATIONS Opinions

5

1	What, bit	3	about	5	sure
2	think, really	4	like		

DEVELOPING WRITING Writing a blog

7

1	goes	3	is making	5	don't like
2	love	4	studied		

8

c

9

1	English	3	games	5	programmes
2	*The Corrections*	4	bands	6	series

10

Students' own answers

11
Students' own answers

VOCABULARY BUILDER QUIZ 7

1
1	Italian	3	Chinese	5	American
2	Mexican	4	Egyptian		

2
1	present	3	running	5	go out
2	writer	4	brown		

3
1	basketball	3	website	5	floor
2	Facebook	4	T-shirt		

4
1	cake	3	prison	5	toy
2	politics	4	business		

5
1	vegetarian	3	sad	5	comfortable
2	famous	4	cheap		

UNIT 8

VOCABULARY Collocations

1

G	L	U	G	N	J	F	N	U	D
R	N	F	E	S	L	Z	L	H	P
M	E	E	T	Y	S	T	P	I	D
X	Z	S	C	H	A	X	T	L	F
S	A	W	O	R	K	M	A	C	A
T	C	D	Q	T	E	L	K	N	Z
U	T	R	A	V	E	L	E	M	U
D	E	Y	N	Z	B	T	W	Z	Q
Y	J	R	S	H	V	Z	P	A	Z
K	I	E	J	Y	M	A	K	E	E

1	get	3	study	5	travel	7	meet
2	take	4	work	6	make		

2
1	get	3	travel	5	make	7	take
2	work	4	study	6	meet		

GRAMMAR Present continuous: all forms

3
1	's	5	working	9	Is
2	coming	6	Are	10	staying
3	's	7	playing		
4	's not	8	're		

4
1 Your sister is going to the gym now.
2 I'm taking a coat with me today.
3 It's not raining in London at the moment.
4 Is your son studying for an exam now?
5 They're not having a party today.
6 Are we waiting for Jan to arrive?
7 Her phone's working.
8 You're not travelling to New York today.

5
1	Are you travelling	4	are they coming
2	am meeting	5	isn't feeling
3	is making	6	isn't raining

DEVELOPING CONVERSATIONS Sending messages

6
1	I'm	3	thank	5	sorry
2	Say	4	hello		

LISTENING

7
1 c 2 a 3 b

8
1	son	5	a Spanish	9	good
2	client	6	is making	10	near
3	can't	7	week		
4	afternoon	8	Adam		

9
1	trip	3	working	5	thirty	7	taxi
2	meet	4	loves	6	walking		

PRONUNCIATION /ɪŋ/

10
ɪŋ

12
Students' own answers

VOCABULARY In the house

1
1	fridge	4	sofa	7	cupboard	10	carpet
2	table	5	bed	8	shelf		
3	shower	6	sink	9	chair		

2
1	bathroom	3	kitchen
2	bedroom	4	living room

GRAMMAR Personal pronouns

3
1	I	2	you	3	it	4	him	5	she	6	them

4
1	him	2	me	3	them	4	you	5	It	6	She

DEVELOPING CONVERSATIONS *Maybe*

5
1	on the train	4	home
2	Saturday night	5	at two o'clock
3	a ten-minute walk		

READING

6
a

7
1 T	2 T	3 DS	4 T	5 T	6 DS	7 F
8 DS	9 F	10 F	11 F	12 T		

Vocabulary Verbs and people

1
1 cleans, a cleaner
2 teach, a teacher
3 drives, a (bus) driver
4 manages, a manager
5 play, a (football) player
6 writes, a writer
7 designs, a designer

2
1 writer
2 cleaner
3 football player
4 teacher
5 manager
6 designer

3
Students' own answers

Pronunciation /g/, /dʒ/ and silent g

4
They are different. The sound of 'g' in *designer* is silent.
/g/: good
/dʒ/: manager
silent g: designer

5
/g/: get, glasses, green
/dʒ/: Argentina, change, gym
silent g: daughter, high, sign

Developing Writing Describing a photo

7
1 *k* in *know*, *w* in *answer*
2 *i* in *business*, *o* in *people*
3 *u* in *guess*, *p* in *cupboard*
4 *g* in *sign*
5 *w* in *writing*
6 *b* in *climb*, *gh* in *high*

9
c

10
1 woman
2 sofa
3 house
4 living room
5 writer
6 moment

11
Students' own answers

12
Students' own answers

Vocabulary Builder Quiz 8

1
1 remember
2 call
3 designs
4 sell
5 leave

2
1 card
2 bag
3 runner
4 parent
5 key

3
1 law
2 factory
3 list
4 fridge
5 dish

4
1 pictures
2 glasses
3 way
4 message
5 company

5
1 b   2 e   3 c   4 a   5 d

UNIT 9

Vocabulary Parts of the body

1
Across
2 back   3 head   5 leg
Down
1 hand   4 eye

2
1 cut, hand
2 broke, leg
3 had, bad cold
4 had, headache
5 felt sick
6 hit, head
7 hurt, back
8 had, in, eye
9 broke, arm

3
Students' own answers

Grammar Time phrases for the past

4
1 days
2 this
3 on
4 minutes
5 last
6 on
7 weeks
8 last
9 this
10 years

5
1 ago   2 This   3 Last   4 few   5 Last

6
Students' own answers

Developing Conversations *Are you feeling better?*

7
1 OK   2 Much   3 bit   4 thanks   5 really

Listening

8
John, Chan, Steven, Joe

9
1 Pam and John
2 John
3 A few months ago
4 Lee
5 He had a bad cold
6 Last week
7 Ivan
8 (the local) bank
9 Three years ago
10 Joe
11 In the kitchen
12 This morning

Pronunciation long and short a and o

13
long *a*, short *a*, long *o*, short *o*

14
long *a*: conversation, safe
short *a*: back, hand
long *o*: cold, broke
short *o*: doctor, hospital

Vocabulary Country and society

1
1 sun
2 university
3 operation
4 countryside
5 war

2
1 snow
2 crime
3 education, teachers
4 environment, water
5 hospital, doctor
6 operation, system

3
Students' own answers

GRAMMAR Quantity

4

1	a lot	3	quite a lot	5	almost no
2	lots	4	some	6	no

5

1	no	3	quite a lot	5	a lot / lots
2	some	4	almost no		

6

1 b   2 a   3 c   4 b   5 c   6 a   7 c

READING

7

education: Japan
environment: Denmark
food: Lebanon
health system: Japan
sport: Denmark
weather: Lebanon

8

1 football
2 Yes, because it's clean.
3 Yes, because it has (beautiful) beaches and lakes.
4 about 7,000 years ago
5 chicken and lamb
6 in the mountains
7 Yes, it has some of the best hospitals in the world.
8 studying hard / going to university
9 because it helps them get better jobs and have better lives

VOCABULARY Meeting and moving

1

1 b   2 h   3 d   4 a   5 f   6 g   7 e   8 c

2

1 To study.
2 How do you know each other?
3 love
4 business
5 university
6 work
7 studied

3

Students' own answers

DEVELOPING CONVERSATIONS *Have you been ...?*

4

1	1 c	2 a	3 b	4 d	
2	1 c	2 d	3 a	4 b	
3	1 a	2 c	3 d	4 b	
4	1 d	2 a	3 c	4 b	5 e

DEVELOPING WRITING Writing an email

5

Beginnings: Dear, / Hello, / Hi,
Endings: Best wishes, / Bye, / Kind regards, / Love, / Write soon,

6

a

7

Students' own answers

8

Students' own answers

VOCABULARY BUILDER QUIZ 9

1

1	air	3	business	5	quite
2	army	4	eye		

2

1	time	3	countryside	5	headache
2	Cup	4	system		

3

1	hand	3	weather	5	summer
2	police	4	street		

4

1 e   2 a   3 c   4 b   5 d

5

1	education	3	operation	5	beautiful
2	safe	4	better		

UNIT 10
VOCABULARY Summer and winter

1

1 S   2 W   3 S   4 W   5 W   6 S   7 W
8 W   9 S   10 S

2

1	minus	5	degrees	9	summer
2	winter	6	wet / windy	10	heating
3	stay	7	windy / wet	11	fire
4	air-conditioning	8	change	12	sunny

3

1 Is it snowing now?
2 It's horrible and cold / cold and horrible today.
3 It rains a lot here. / It rains here a lot.
4 It was very wet here last winter.
5 Did it rain in London yesterday?

VOCABULARY EXTRA *like*

4

1 a   2 b   3 b   4 a   5 a

GRAMMAR Future: *am/are/is going*

5

1 e   2 f   3 a   4 b   5 c   6 d

6

1 's	2 'm	3 're	4 's	5 're	6 're

7

1	're/are going to get	4	is going to stay
2	'm/am going to do	5	're/are going to take
3	is going to have	6	is going to play

DEVELOPING CONVERSATIONS *I think so / I don't think so*

8

1	Is	3	don't	5	so
2	going	4	Do	6	think

9

Students' own answers

LISTENING

10

1 d   2 c   3 e   4 b   5 a

11

1 F   2 T   3 F   4 T   5 F   6 T   7 F
8 T   9 F   10 T

VOCABULARY Entertainment

1

1 fair   3 circus   5 classical concert
2 match   4 festival

2

1 band   3 concerts   5 exhibition
2 play   4 shows

3

1 T   2 F   3 F   4 T   5 F   6 T

4

Students' own answers

DEVELOPING CONVERSATIONS Deciding what to do

5

1 Yeah   4 OK   7 'd
2 How   5 about   8 'll meet
3 'd prefer   6 really

PRONUNCIATION Long and short vowel sounds: *e* and *u*

7

long *e*, short *e*, long *u*, short *u*

8

long *e*: he, meet
short *e*: help, spend
long *u*: June, music
short *u*: club, sun

READING

10

✓ a, b, c; ✗ d

11

1 August   7 Three weeks
2 Edinburgh, Scotland   8 sometimes warm and dry,
3 1947   usually it rains
4 Eight   9 the Royal Mile
5 3,398   10 Next Friday
6 Comedy

13

Students' own answers

VOCABULARY National and international news

1

1 b   2 d   3 e   4 c   5 a

2

1 died, a heart attack   6 fire
2 had, baby   7 married
3 accident   8 scored
4 build   9 factory
5 spend

GRAMMAR Past forms review

3

E	Q	N	W	I	P	V	W	Y	N
T	S	E	A	M	M	H	H	A	L
O	F	W	Q	G	V	A	R	Z	D
O	I	W	N	E	L	P	W	C	E
K	N	G	O	T	C	P	A	O	C
K	I	A	C	W	L	E	S	P	I
R	S	A	T	O	O	N	Z	E	D
K	H	D	R	N	S	E	L	N	E
L	E	W	C	R	T	D	K	E	D
S	D	S	T	O	P	P	E	D	D

4 and 5

be	was	Ir
decide	decided	R
finish	finished	R
get	got	Ir
happen	happened	R
lose	lost	Ir
open	opened	R
stop	stopped	R
take	took	Ir
win	won	Ir

6

1 a cut   b talked
2 a came   b helped
3 a cost   b tried
4 a spent   b used
5 a met   b played

DEVELOPING WRITING Writing a postcard

7

1 clean   3 famous   5 interesting
2 warm   4 old

8

Students should underline: beautiful, small, great, hot, sunny, beautiful, busy, warm, interesting, local, fun, main, cold
Beginning: Hello, Beatrice!
Ending: Bye for now, Noel

9

Students should tick a, b, d, e, g and write notes with their own ideas.

10

Students' own answers

VOCABULARY BUILDER QUIZ 10

1

1 cost   3 play   5 fun
2 main   4 like

2

1 conditioning/con   4 room
2 music   5 attack
3 show

3

1 stay warm   4 get wet
2 win the match   5 close the club
3 die in an accident

4

1 c   2 d   3 b   4 e   5 a

5

1 election   2 windy   3 skiing   4 discussion

UNIT 11

VOCABULARY Months

1

1 January	5 May	9 September
2 February	6 June	10 October
3 March	7 July	11 November
4 April	8 August	12 December

2

1	a in	b	during
2	a beginning	b	first
3	a middle	b	second or third
4	a end	b	last

3

1 c   2 g   3 a   4 h   5 b   6 e   7 d   8 f

4

1 during	3 middle	5 last
2 beginning	4 end	

5

1 the first	4 the twenty-fourth
2 the fourth	5 the twenty-sixth
3 the sixteenth	

GRAMMAR Questions review

6

1 Does Dan want to come to the cinema?
2 Why wasn't Bill at the party yesterday?
3 Can you come to my parents' party?
4 How old is your sister going to be?
5 Who are you going to dinner with?
6 Are you doing anything to celebrate?
7 What did you get your husband for his birthday?
8 Did you go anywhere last summer?

7

1 Why	3 Who	5 Where	7 Is	9 Did
2 How	4 Can	6 Does	8 What	

8

1 c, How old is she going to be
2 e, Who are you going with
3 a, Can you help me with my homework
4 d, Did she and her husband do anything to celebrate
5 b, Why was it horrible

DEVELOPING CONVERSATIONS Invitations

9

1 Can, check	3 going, come, dates
2 Do, love, day, can't	4 Maybe, diary

LISTENING

11

a birthday party
an anniversary
a conference
a barbecue

12

1	Luigi's	8	3 pm (in the afternoon)
2	Italian	9	14 New Road
3	South Street	10	Tokyo
4	9th September	11	26th September
5	ten	12	29th September
6	20th September	13	27th September
7	barbecue		

VOCABULARY Life events

1

1	of a heart	4	a degree	7	divorced
	attack	5	an online shop	8	married
2	university	6	interested		
3	a new life		in art		

2

1 was born	3	have	5	live
2 start	4	get	6	become

3

Students' own answers

GRAMMAR Explaining when: time phrases

4

1 After	3 In	5 after
2 in	4 when	6 When

5

1 When	3 when	5 in	7 When
2 after	4 after	6 in	8 in

6

1 g   2 c   3 a   4 d   5 h   6 f   7 e   8 b

READING

7

1 inventor   2 nurse

8

1 the third	5	the twelfth
2 1876	6	sick
3 Canada	7	clean
4 phones	8	so she visited sick people

9

1 T
2 F, He moved to Canada in 1870.
3 T
4 F, He died in the summer.
5 F, Florence Nightingale moved to England with her family in 1821.
6 F, She didn't go to school when she was a child.
7 T
8 F, She died in 1910.

PRONUNCIATION /i/, /ɪ/ and /aɪ/

11

/i/, /ɪ/ and /aɪ/

12

/i/: hungry, history
/ɪ/: with, busy, prison
/aɪ/: outside, night, died, why

VOCABULARY History

1

1	a	high	b	big
2	a	fought	b	killed
3	a	repaired	b	damaged
4	a	main	b	capital
5	a	castle	b	wall
6	a	queen	b	king
7	a	century	b	year

2

1	high	4	walls	7	protect
2	centuries	5	king	8	damaged, repair
3	fought	6	killed	9	capital

GRAMMAR Explaining why: *because* and *so*

3

1	a	because	b	so
2	a	because	b	so
3	a	so	b	because
4	a	so	b	because

4

1 d   2 e   3 a   4 f   5 b   6 c

DEVELOPING WRITING Writing an autobiography

5

b

6

1	was born	3	finished school	5 got married
2	1988	4	2007	

7–9

Students' own answers

VOCABULARY BUILDER QUIZ 11

1

1	middle	4	second
2	queen	5	prison
3	anniversary		

2

1	was	4	moved
2	got	5	fought
3	celebrated		

3

1	grandma/grandmother	4	countryside
2	boyfriend	5	anywhere
3	online		

4

1 b   2 d   3 c   4 e   5 a

5

1	lucky	4	interested
2	angry	5	somewhere
3	independent		

UNIT 12

VOCABULARY Offering solutions

1

1	working	4	strong	7	wrong
2	low	5	heavy	8	empty
3	broken	6	lost		

2

1	carry	3	show	5	repair
2	charger	4	lend	6	seat

GRAMMAR *I'll*

3

1 e   2 f   3 a   4 g   5 c   6 b   7 d

4

d, f, g
Suggested solutions
d Throw it in the bin / I'll get them to make another one. /
   We can go to another café if you like.
f Do you want to look for another restaurant?
g Come to my room and watch mine.

5

1	I'll send	3	I'll lend	5 I'll check
2	I'll repair	4	I'll go	

DEVELOPING CONVERSATIONS Checking and thanking

6

1	1 c	2 a	3 d	4 b	5 e
2	1 b	2 e	3 c	4 a	5 d
3	1 c	2 e	3 b	4 d	5 a

LISTENING

7

1 b   2 b

8

Students should tick: 2, 4, 5, 8

9

2 c   4 e   5 f   8 g

PRONUNCIATION long and short vowel sounds review

10

long *a*: place, safe
long *e*: me, we
long *o*: home, hope
long *u*: computer, rule
short *a*: back, taxi
short *e*: get, send
short *o*: chocolate, contact
short *u*: stuff, sunny

Vocabulary Extra Gifts

1

Across
5	toy	6	sweets	7	jewellery

Down
1	sculpture	3	painting	6	shirt
2	flowers	4	computer		

2
1	painting	4	chocolates	7	money
2	home-made	5	book	8	lovely
3	T-shirt	6	sculpture		

3

1 b   2 a   3 b   4 a   5 b

Grammar Explaining purpose: *for* or *to*

4

1 ✓

2 anywhere ~~to~~ **for** some

3 flowers ~~for~~ **to** say

4 a good place ~~to~~ **for** a

5 ✓

6 the best place ~~for~~ **to** go

5

1 for, for   2 to, for, to   3 to, for   4 for

Developing Writing Writing a letter about a problem

6

1 First   2 Then   3 In the end

7

Beginning: Dear Sir or Madam,
Ending: Yours faithfully, Gabriella Hollis
1 First   2 Then   3 end

8

Students should tick 1, 4, 5, 6 and write their own notes

9

Students' own answers

Vocabulary Leaving and saying goodbye

1
1	enjoyed	4	hope	7	need
2	forgot	5	missed		
3	Give	6	order		

2
1	kind	4	contact	7	lovely, care
2	quick	5	everything	8	Thanks
3	journey	6	phone		

3

1 F   2 T   3 T   4 F   5 T   6 T   7 F   8 T

Grammar Telling people to do things: Imperatives

4

1 Give me a call when you're home. I will.
2 Don't forget to call us. I won't.
3 Have a good journey. I will.
4 Don't work too hard. I won't.
5 Don't forget your plane ticket. I won't.
6 Get some rest on your holiday. I will.
You can answer with *OK.* in all of them.

5
1	Help	4	Say	7	Don't ask
2	Don't forget	5	Go	8	Don't work, Get
3	Don't be	6	Hurry		

Reading

6

Students should tick: 1, 3, 4, 5

7

1 flowers   2 money   3 sweets   4 pens

8

1 Anything they can cut their hand with.
2 Because they think a gift like that means you want to 'cut' being their friend.
3 After the 'giver' leaves.
4 right
5 three
6 Brazilian people
7 Japanese people
8 Indian people

Vocabulary Builder Quiz 12

1
1	low	3	forget	5	quick
2	empty	4	lovely		

2
1	theatre	3	a call	5	space
2	a seat	4	a brother		

3
1	up	3	out	5	in
2	care	4	other		

4

1 b   2 c   3 a   4 e   5 d

5

1 lost
2 charger
3 hungry
4 useful
5 definitely